DEEP
RHYTHM
AND THE
RIDDLE
OF
ETERNAL
LIFE

DEEP
RHYTHM
AND THE
RIDDLE
OF
ETERNAL
LIFE

JOHN S. DUNNE

University of Notre Dame Press

Notre Dame, Indiana

Manufactured in the United States of America

Title Page and CD art: JupiterImages © 2007

Library of Congress Cataloging-in-Publication Data

Dunne, John S., 1929–
Deep rhythm and the riddle of eternal life / John S. Dunne.
p. cm.
Includes bibliographical references and index.
ISBN-13: 978-0-268-02596-0 (pbk. : alk. paper)
ISBN-10: 0-268-02596-7 (pbk. : alk. paper)
1. Death—Religious aspects—Christianity.
2. Future life—Christianity.   I. Title.
BS2545.D45D86   2008
236'.1—dc22
                          2008000414

∞ *The paper in this book meets the guidelines for permanence and
durability of the Committee on Production Guidelines for Book
Longevity of the Council on Library Resources.*

CONTENTS

PREFACE

Is death an event of life? Is death lived through?
No, Wittgenstein has said, "Death is not an event of life.
Death is not lived through."[1] But what if the answer is Yes,
it *is* an event of life, it *is* lived through? If it is, as has been
assumed in most civilizations but our own, and in our own
too before the time of the Black Death, then we face "the
riddle of eternal life," as I call it here. I see the answer to
the riddle in the Gospel of John with its three great
metaphors, life and light and love. And I see the meaning
of the metaphors in "deep rhythm," as I call it here, the
deep rhythm of rest in the restlessness of the heart.

Life and light and love, the three metaphors, form
a great circle in the Gospel of John, from and of and towards God, as in the words of the old Bedouin to Lawrence
of Arabia, "The love is from God and of God and towards
God."[2] Eternal life then is the great circle of life and light
and love. There is a far point on the circle, though, farther-
most from God, and so as Wendell Berry says in a poem,
"Even love must pass through loneliness,"[3] and we could
say too, "Even light must pass through darkness" and "Even
life must pass through death." And so "the words of eternal

life" in the Gospel speak of life and light and love but also of life passing through death, of light passing through darkness, of love passing through loneliness. So too Christ, embodying the life and the light and the love, passes through death and darkness and loneliness.

Deep rhythm then, the deep rhythm of eternal life, is a rest in the restlessness of the heart. It is like the poise of a whirling gyroscope. The restlessness of the heart appears in passing through loneliness, through darkness, through death. Rest in restlessness is an acceptance of the restless movement of the heart from image to image, a dwelling in that movement. It is love in the loneliness, light in the darkness, life in the dying. "Our heart is restless until it rests in you,"[4] Saint Augustine's saying in the beginning of his *Confessions*, seems to describe this process of passing through loneliness, through darkness, through death, and coming to repose in life and light and love. "Wisdom is repose in light,"[5] Joseph Joubert says. It is repose in life and light and love, I want to say, and that is the meaning of "Our heart is restless until it rests in you." Wisdom is repose in God, and that is rest in the restlessness of the heart, "at the still point of the turning world."[6]

Life and light and love then, and deep rhythm are metaphors of eternal life. Rest in the restlessness of the heart is the meaning of the metaphors. If we take the restlessness of the heart to be the stream of consciousness as it goes from image to image, rest in the restlessness is a relation to the things of life flowing in the stream of consciousness and so is not just part of the flux but is or can be something lasting and enduring. If "we all have within us a center of stillness surrounded by silence,"[7] as Dag Hammarskjöld says, this rest can describe dwelling in our center of stillness. Can it also describe "eternal rest," life after death? I am hoping it can, as if life after death is the same as what is now our inner life.

So when we speak of deep rhythm and the riddle of eternal life, we are speaking of metaphors, but they are "cognitive metaphors." They are images, but there is insight into the images. What is more, there is a metaphor that combines all into one, and that is Tolkien's image of the road that goes ever on. "He used often to say there was only one Road; that it was like a great river: its springs were at every doorstep, and every path was its tributary."[8] It suggests "the road not taken" in life rejoins the road taken. For me the road not taken is the way of music and the road taken is the way of words, but in these later years the roads have rejoined for me, and that is what I try to illustrate here at the end with my "Symphony of Songs." The rejoining of the roads is my deep rhythm and my answer to the riddle of eternal life.

I want to thank Quinn SmithPillari, who sang my "Symphony of Songs" with me accompanying her on the piano at Notre Dame in the spring of 2003, and Dustin George Miller, who recorded it on compact disc, and the University of Notre Dame Press for bringing it out. I also wrote an orchestral version for soprano and string orchestra, but that has not yet been performed. The songs are from my previous song cycles but are combined here in three symphonic movements.

A QUESTION
OF HEART'S DESIRE

> If I must die someday, what can I do to satisfy my desire to live?
>
> —my question in my first book,
> *The City of the Gods*

In a strange story by David Lindsay, *A Voyage to Arcturus*, there is a rhythm that can be heard again and again, a drumbeat that is first heard over the sound of surf on the North Sea. It is the rhythm, I suppose, of a deeper life that can live on through death. "Only try to hear it more and more distinctly,"[1] Maskull, the main character of the story, is told. I heard that the Velvet Underground, a rock group in the sixties, was planning a rock opera based on the story when the group disbanded. I can imagine the beat and the strobe lights of the rock opera. The deep rhythm of eternal life, I suppose, can be heard not with the ears but only with the mind. "Only try to hear it more and more distinctly . . ."

There is a dualism of good and evil, Krag and Crystalman in the story, that repels me, as I look for a sense of eternal life. My question is "If I must die someday, what can I do to satisfy my desire to live?" a life-affirming question, as it seems to me, and I look for a depth of life, a deep rhythm of life that can encompass death and survive it, rather than death as the horrible Crystalman grin in Lindsay's story. It is true, I didn't think of the question till I had considered many answers to death in writing my first book, *The City of the Gods.* I thought of the question at the end and put it into the conclusion and into the preface, the last parts I wrote. So it can give the impression that I knew what I was doing. Now, though, I do begin with it and I imagine it will be transformed as I write on, maybe into an answer that is the deep rhythm of eternal life.

Rhythm is the element that is common to words and music. My question is in words, but there are answers in music, in song and dance. It is a question of desire, of heart's desire, and if the answer is in the rhythm of our lives, the basic metaphor is that of the heartbeat. One answer is to live in the present, as Wittgenstein puts it, "eternal life belongs to those who live in the present,"[2] for if I live in the present, I am living without regret of the past or fear of the future, even fear of death. Another answer is to live in a consciousness of my life as a whole, in freedom from the past and openness to the future, open even to death, so my life is "being toward death," as Heidegger says, and "freedom toward death."[3]

These answers of twentieth-century philosophers, even that of Wittgenstein, who speaks here of eternity but identifies it with the present moment, are answers within the horizon of time, "the possible horizon," as Heidegger says, "for any understanding whatsoever of being."[4] But if time, as Plato says, is "a changing image of eternity," then we can go beyond the horizon of time to eternity, as in Henry Vaughan's poem,

I saw Eternity the other night,
Like a great ring of pure and endless light,
All calm, as it was bright.[5]

It is here in the great circle of eternity that we may find the answer to the heart's desire. Or if we look for it in time, the answer is in time as "a changing image of eternity."

A Quest of Eternal Life

My own quest of eternal life took me all the way from Gilgamesh to Heidegger, covering the whole span of recorded history. It was a quest like that of Gilgamesh, but the figures I met on the quest were historical figures instead of the figures of legend. The meetings, nevertheless, were very similar. Gilgamesh met figures who told him to turn back and embrace a human happiness, that eternal life was reserved for the immortal gods. I met figures who tried to find immortality in noble deeds that would be forever remembered or in running the gamut of experience and living life to the full or in making life their own and becoming free toward death. It was only in "the words of eternal life" in the Gospel that I found the hope of eternal life I was looking for. All other answers seemed to fail. "Lord, to whom shall we go?" Peter says to Jesus in the Gospel of John. "You have the words of eternal life."[6]

Where to go from here? Now I seek for an understanding of eternal life. "Faith seeking understanding" (*fides quaerens intellectum*), as Saint Anselm calls it following Saint Augustine, leads you on a quest again, faith in eternal life seeking understanding of eternal life. This quest is a "repetition," as Kierkegaard uses the term, of the quest of Gilgamesh on a deeper level. Gilgamesh journeyed toward the sunrise, according to the ancient epic. "This is the point where the two ends of the circular world meet," as Kleist says in his marvelous essay "On the Marionette Theatre."[7] We must journey again towards that point in order to find an understanding of eternal life. What we are likely to find is the great circle of life and light and love that is set forth in the Gospel of John or in the words of the old Bedouin to Lawrence of Arabia, "The love is from God and of God and towards God."[8]

What path are we to follow to come to this point of understanding eternal life? I imagine it will be what Kleist calls *the path taken by the soul of the dancer.*[9] When he says this, Kleist is thinking of the marionette theatre, how the puppeteer dances when the puppets dance. I think of the words "David danced before the Lord with all his might,"[10] thinking of eternal life as loving with all your heart and with all your soul and with all your might. If eternal life does prove to be the great circle of life and light and love, the love that is "from God and of God and towards God," then it does make sense to follow "the path taken by the soul of the dancer," as in a circle dance in which the dancers join hands and move in a circle, for instance where women form a circle and move clockwise and men form a circle around them and move counterclockwise (and the man and woman opposite one another when the music stops become partners in the next dance).

It is true, Kleist envisions the puppets moving in a straight line. The controlling string, as he imagines it, is fastened to their center of gravity, so when they are moved in a straight line their limbs describe circles. No doubt, dance is a metaphor here, a "conceptual metaphor" I would say, borrowing the term from cognitive science. The puppeteer dances when the puppets dance. So it is, when others dance to my music, I dance when they dance. Where then does "the path taken by the soul of the dancer" lead us? Does it lead us into the great circle of life and light and love?

"Grace appears most purely," Kleist concludes "in the human form which either has no consciousness or an infinite consciousness."[11] As he understands it, "This is the point where the two ends of the circular world meet." And he asks "Does that mean we must eat again of the tree of knowledge in order to return to the state of innocence?" And he concludes "Of course, but that's the final chapter in the history of the world." According to this, our quest leads us back to our unconscious beginnings, only we come back consciously and to a greater consciousness. The circular path we follow is that of a circle dance, but we don't necessarily make it back to the very beginning. Instead, when the music stops, the man and woman opposite each other become partners in the next dance. Still, if the music does not stop for us, I believe, we keep coming back to the very beginning and we find ourselves in the great circle of life and light and love.

All this is metaphor, but what does it mean? As I understand it, the deep loneliness of the human condition, the loneliness we feel in the face of death, becomes the love, and thus is illumined, becomes the light, and thus proves to be the deep life. "So the darkness becomes the light," as T. S. Eliot says, "and the stillness the dancing."[12] The deep loneliness is already there in our experience, but coming back to the beginning enables us to recognize it as life and light and love. Or vice-versa, recognizing it is coming back to the beginning. As it is, we experience it as being alone and longing to be unalone, and the longing to be unalone is our heart's longing, our heart's desire.

There is a joy in the love, just as there is a sadness in the loneliness. According to Spinoza, love of God is simply joy at the thought of God,[13] for me joy at the thought of being on a journey with God, joy that God is my companion on the way. For me it is the joy of God-with-us (Emmanuel). So when the loneliness of the human condition becomes the love of God, as I experience it, the sadness passes into the joy, and it does so again and again each time I remember God, each time I remember joy. There is the sadness of mortal men and women, the sadness "if I must die someday," and it is transformed into the joy of "what I can do to satisfy my desire to live," and what I can do, I am thinking, is walk with God.

"Enoch walked with God; and he was not, for God took him."[14] I always think of this passage in Genesis when I think of walking with God. It has the hint, and more than a hint, of eternal life in those words "and he was not, for God took him." Seeing my life as a journey with God in time, I am hoping it can be said also of me, "He walked with God; and he was not, for God took him." The sadness of our mortality keeps coming back to me, and I have again and again to invoke the joy of God-with-us, often reciting George Herbert's mystical song,

> Come my joy, my love, my heart,
> Such a joy as none can move,
> Such a love as none can part,
> Such a heart as joys in love.[15]

Going from loneliness to love of God, ever and again on my quest of eternal life, I am going from the Many to the One, from many desires to one heart's desire, as in the biblical imperative, "Seek peace, and ensue it."[16] For my loneliness, by itself, can move in many directions, seeking intimacy with many different individuals. If the deep longing in our loneliness is really a longing for God, the longing does not already know this but has to learn it through the experience of life and the illumination that comes of faith in eternal life. Thus Tolstoy in his late years wrote "God is my desire" in his diary, but he could not easily explain that to Max Gorky, who saw those words in the diary.[17] I want to say that too, "God is my desire," for I can feel the peace in that standpoint, but I can also feel the tug of the many desires pulling me in all directions.

If I follow "the path taken by the soul of the dancer," I go from the Many to the One and join the dance around the One that Plotinus describes, "And we are always around it (the One) but do not always look at it," he says, "it is like a choral dance . . . but when we do look to him (God), then we are at our goal and at rest and do not sing out of tune as we dance our god-inspired dance around him."[18] As I understand it, this dance is simply a metaphor for dwelling in our center of stillness. This, I believe, is what Plotinus means by being "alone with the Alone,"[19] not being cut off from everyone and everything else but rather joining everyone and everything in the dance around the One.

"We all have within us a center of stillness surrounded by silence,"[20] Dag Hammarskjöld says. This is the opening sentence of the brochure he wrote for the Meditation Room at the U.N. We can experience this center of stillness in ourselves when we are outdoors in the beauty of nature, among the giant redwood trees or by the shore of the sea, and we can experience it simply when we are sitting quietly in a room. "And we are always around it but do not always look at it," this center of stillness, as Plotinus says, "but when we do look to him (God), then we are at our goal and at rest and do not sing out of tune as we dance our god-inspired dance around him." As I understand it, the center of stillness we all have within us is what I am calling "the heart," the place where all the dimensions of life meet, and the presence of God to us is the surrounding silence.

There is a clash of images here, Plotinus has God or the One in our center of stillness and I have the divine presence in the surrounding silence. God is there in both images. I suppose it is like God in the heart, Atman, and God in the universe, Brahman in Hinduism, and Atman and Brahman are one, according to the Upanishads. God in our center of stillness is God in the heart, and God in the surrounding silence is God in the universe, and it is one and the same God. The dance image is affected: we dance around God in the center, but God dances with us in the surrounding silence.

Walking with God on "the path taken by the soul of the dancer," I am walking in the great circle of life and light and love. No doubt this is a metaphor. Is it more than a metaphor? "I came from the Father and have come into the world; again, I am leaving the world and going to the Father," Jesus tells his disciples in the Gospel of John, and they reply "Ah, now you are speaking plainly, not in any figure!"[21] Walking with God on "the path taken by the soul of the dancer," I am on a path that comes from God and returns to God, that of the great circle of life and light and love. If I say this, am I speaking plainly, not in any figure? The circular path is "from God and of God and towards God." Because it is "from God" I came from God and have come into the world; because it is "of God" I am walking on the path with God; and because it is "towards God" I am leaving the world and going to God. What Christ is saying, as Meister Eckhart always says, I can say too.

Does this take away the uniqueness of Christ? No, for it is "through him, with him, in him,"[22] as is said in the Eucharistic prayer, that I have all I am. If I am "from God," it is because he has come "from the Father" and has "come into the world," and if I live "towards God" rather than simply towards death, it is because of him "leaving the world and going to the Father," and if I am "of God" and walk with God, it is because he is "God-with-us" (Emmanuel). It is the love that is "from God and of God and towards God," and so it is by being caught up in the love that my life acquires his "whence" and "whither."

"Existence is God" (*Esse est Deus*), Meister Eckhart says, and there is one existence (*unum esse*) in Christ the Word made flesh, he says following Saint Thomas Aquinas, and so also in us, he concludes, like Wittgenstein saying "It is not *how* things are in the world that is mystical, but *that* it exists."[23] So if the wonder of existence is "the mystical," then all the things that Eckhart says make sense, that existence is God, that this is the existence of Christ, and that through and with and in Christ it is also our existence. It is the wonder of existence, I think, that Heidegger has in mind when he says "we are too late for the gods and too early for Being."[24]

I suppose we are "too early" because we take existence for granted. The gods go with the wonder of *how* things are in the world, God with the wonder *that* it exists. We are too late for the gods with our scientific account of *how* things are in the world. We are too early for Being in that we are not thinking back (*andenken*) to Being but are caught up instead in representational thinking (*vorstellendes denken*), or so Heidegger would say. If we no longer took existence for granted, on the other hand, then thinking would become thanking, as he says "Thinking is thanking" (*denken ist danken*),[25] quoting the mystics of the seventeenth century. A thinking that is thanking is also what Wittgenstein calls "the mystical," "not *how* things are in the world . . . but *that* it exists."

Does this make God the least common denominator of things to say, as Meister Eckhart does, *Esse est Deus?* No, that would be taking existence as belonging simply to "*how* things are in the world." Instead existence is "the mystical," the wonder "*that* it exists." Saint Thomas Aquinas calls God *ipsum esse,* but he argues in his *Summa Contra Gentiles* that God is not the *esse formale omnium.*[26] As I understand it, the wonder of existence is one thing, the least common denominator of things is another. I suppose everything here depends on a thinking that is thanking. If I see the existence of things as the least common denominator, I take it for granted. If I perceive the wonder of existence, then my thinking becomes thanking.

I think Meister Eckhart saying *Esse est Deus* means what Saint Thomas Aquinas means saying God is *ipsum esse subsistens,* "subsistent existence itself," only Eckhart understands God to be giving his own existence to all things, creating them, and giving it to us too as revealed in Christ, especially when Christ says "I am." In those "I am" sayings, sometimes translated "It is I" and "I am he," Christ is speaking of the Shekinah, as my friend David Daube used to say,[27] the divine presence in the world. The presence of God, I believe, is what Meister Eckhart means too when he says *Esse est Deus,* God is present to all things, giving them existence.

Understanding then the wonder of existence with Meister Eckhart as the divine presence in the world, and saying all that is said of Christ can be said of us through and with and in Christ, we are in effect saying existence is "from God and of God and towards God," echoing the words of the old Bedouin to Lawrence of Arabia, "The love is from God and of God and towards God." So the great circle of existence is the great circle of life and light and love and thus the great circle of eternal life. It all depends on thinking that is thanking, perceiving existence not as the least common denominator of things but as the wonder of existence, the mystical, not *how* things are in the world but *that* it exists.

Have we proved too much, though, talking of existence and the divine presence in the world, not just that we can participate in eternal life but that the world is eternal? "Is some riddle solved by my surviving for ever?" Wittgenstein asks. "Is not this eternal life as much of a riddle as our present life?"[28] Let us consider now this riddle of our present life and eternal life.

The Riddle of Eternal Life

"When the answer cannot be put into words, neither can the question be put into words," Wittgenstein says. "*The riddle* does not exist. If a question can be framed at all, it is also *possible* to answer it."[29] What he means by riddle (*Rätsel* in German) is an unanswerable question. If we take it to mean instead simply an unanswered question, then there are three riddles here, I think, the riddle

(A) of eternal life,
(B) of dark light, and
(C) of love shown and withdrawn,

corresponding to the three great metaphors in the Gospel of John, life and light and love.

There is a cluster of questions here about divine action. I think of God as illumining the mind and kindling the heart. So I am inclined to think of God as creating in the same way, "Let there be light," knowing and loving things into being. "God is spirit,"[30] as is said in the Gospel of John, and so God acts spiritually. The riddle of eternal life then is the question whether our own life of knowledge and love, the life of the spirit, is capable of enduring death and surviving it. Even that sentence "Existence is God" or "God is subsistent existence itself," I take to mean "God is spirit," as if to say to be and to know and to love are one and the same thing when you are speaking of God. It is like saying "I think therefore I am," I know and I love therefore I am. Can our life of knowing and loving then, our life of the spirit, survive our death and live on forever?

Dark light is a second riddle here, closely related to that of eternal life. What I mean by "dark light" is God illumining our minds and yet remaining unseen, like physical light passing unseen through space until it strikes an object and then becomes visible, or what becomes visible is the object illumined. So it is with divine light illumining our minds without us seeing God. Arthur Zajonc, a physicist studying the quantum theory of light and comparing the experience of spiritual light, calls this "catching the light."[31] Perhaps this is why eternal life is also a riddle. We can experience the life of the spirit, the hope, the peace, the friends, the intelligence that belong to the life of the spirit. To know, though, that the life of the spirit is eternal and survives death would be like seeing the light itself and not just the objects that are illumined by the light.

Love shown and withdrawn is a third riddle here, connected with the sense of mystery. "That which shows itself and at the same time withdraws is the essential trait of what we call the mystery," Heidgger says, speaking of the mystery in technology ("The meaning pervading technology hides itself").[32] It is true, though, of the mystery that shows and withdraws in eternal life and in dark light and in the love that is from and of and towards God. "The inner voice of love," Henri Nouwen calls it, describing his own "journey through anguish to freedom."[33] There is this tantalizing experience of love shown and withdrawn in human friendship that discloses the mystery of life and light and love. The riddle is the mystery.

It is the great circle of life and light and love that is the answer to all three of these riddles. Hope and peace and friends and intelligence, all the life of the spirit, locate me on this great circle that circles from God to God and is of God who is spirit. If I am on the great circle, walking with God, I have the hope of eternal life, the intelligence of dark light, the friends of love shown and withdrawn, all the riddles of life and light and love, but the answer to the riddles is in the peace, as Dante says, "his will is our peace" (*la sua voluntate e nostra pace*).[34] If "we all have within us a center of stillness surrounded by silence," we all have within us the center of the great circle of life and light and love, and there is our peace. If the center is a moving center like the moving eye of a storm, we are moving on a journey in time and the surrounding silence is the surrounding presence of

God with us on the journey. All this again is metaphor, but the hope and the peace and the friends and the intelligence are real.

Speaking of the here and hereafter, Rilke says "The true pattern of life extends through both domains, the blood with the greatest circuit runs through both: there is neither a This-side nor a That-side but a single great unity in which the beings who transcend us, the angels, have their habitation."[35] His metaphor here is that of the circulation of the blood, flowing through the arteries from the heart and returning through the veins to the heart. God is the heart of the world, and the circulation of life and light and love is from God to God. Death, according to this metaphor, is not a going out of existence but a going to the heart of the world, a return through the veins to the heart. So if God is the heart of the world, death is a going home to God.

"Death is the side of life that is turned away from, and unillumined by us," Rilke says in the same letter: "we must try to achieve the greatest possible consciousness of our being which is at home in both these immeasurable realms and is nourished inexhaustibly by both." I wrote a song called "Dark Light":

> Why is it dark at night?
> —a thousand stars
> are like a thousand suns!
> Why is it dark before me,
> if your light
> shines on my path?
> I can know more
> than I can tell
> of light and darkness,
> for if your eyes open,

there is light,
if your eyes close,
then there is dark,
but light inside my heart.[36]

It is especially death, "the side of life that is turned away from and unillumined by us," that is dark to us, "there is dark, but light inside my heart." The kindling of the heart leads to the illumining of the mind, and what is "unillumined by us" becomes illumined.

It is the kindling of the heart that is the answer also to the third riddle, that of love shown and withdrawn. "He did not tell Gandalf, but as he was speaking a great desire to follow Bilbo flamed up in his heart—to follow Bilbo, and even perhaps to find him again," Tolkien says of Frodo at the beginning of his adventure. "It was so strong that it overcame his fear: he could almost have run out there and then down the road without his hat, as Bilbo had done on a similar morning long ago."[37] There is a kindling of the heart at the thought of a journey with God in time that can overcome fear and overcome sadness too, the sadness of a friend's love withdrawn. For the love of God is simply joy at the thought of God, as Spinoza says, joy at the thought of being on a journey with God, I would say, and it can be so strong that it overcomes fear and sadness with what Meister Eckhart calls "wandering joy,"[38] the joy of being on a journey with God.

There is a connection between the inner peace and the inner light of the life of the spirit. I can see this in the musical settings of Mozart in the last year of his life ("Eternal rest give them, Lord, and let perpetual light shine on them") (*Requiem aeternam dona eis Domine et lux perpetua luceat eis*). The connection appears in the *Ave Verum*, written in the last summer of his life, in the *Requiem* and in *The Magic Flute,* his last major works. "Eternal rest" (*Requiem aeternam*) is the inner peace, and "perpetual light" (*lux perpetua*) is the inner light. As the Quakers understand it, the inner light gives spiritual enlightenment, moral guidance, and religious assurance to those who seek it in faith. If we take the inner light this way, then "perpetual light" shines already in this life, and "eternal rest" exists already in this life as inner peace. The Freemasonry of *The Magic Flute,* looking to this life, and the Catholicism of the *Ave Verum* and the *Requiem,* looking to the life beyond, come together in this sense of an inner life that can survive death.

Spiritual enlightenment, I suppose, as it comes from the inner light, is the answer to Saint Augustine's prayer in his *Soliloquies,* "May I know me! May I know thee!" (*noverim me, noverim te*).[39] I suppose too it is already enlightenment just to pray that prayer. For often there is an answer just in the turn of a question. That is how it is here, for we are a mystery to ourselves, unable to leap over our own shadow, and so praying "May I know me! May I know thee!" we acknowledge the mystery and the connection between knowing ourselves and knowing God. It is "the cloud of unknowing in the which a soul is oned with God."[40] Praying to know me and to know thee, I am "oned with God" in "the cloud of unknowing," and this is spiritual enlightenment, a knowing of my unknowing, and brings me closer to God than any supposed knowing of God.

Moral guidance, I think, as it comes from the inner light, is the answer to Newman's prayer,

Lead, Kindly Light,
Amid the encircling gloom,
Lead Thou me on!

The night is dark,
And I am far from home—
Lead Thou me on!
Keep Thou my feet;
I do not ask to see the distant scene—
One step enough for me.[41]

Here again there is an answer already in the prayer itself, the wisdom of not asking "to see the distant scene," the remote future, but only the next step, "One step enough for me," the realization that "The future—any future—was simply one step at a time out of the heart."[42]

Religious assurance, I believe, as it comes from the inner light, is the answer to Donne's prayer,

I have a sin of fear, that when I have spun
    My last thread, I shall perish on the shore;
Swear by thyself, that at my death thy Son
    Shall shine as he shines now, and heretofore;
        And, having done that, thou hast done,
            I fear no more.[43]

The answer is there in the prayer, the Sun shining and the Son shining, the Son of God, that is, as in the pun there, and there is also the pun, Thou hast done and Thou hast Donne. I just read a review of a book called *The Dream of Eternal Life*, written from the viewpoint of molecular biology.[44] Religious assurance, though, is more than a dream of eternal life. It is the assurance of the Sun shining and the Son shining.

Spiritual enlightenment, moral guidance, and religious assurance, therefore, as they come from the inner light are the answer to prayer, and I am led to think of turning the truth of a life into prayer, as Goethe speaks in his autobiography (*Poetry and Truth in My Life*) of turning the truth of a life into poetry. We all have a continual conversation with ourselves, a conversation about our hopes and fears. Prayer, as I understand it, means letting that conversation with ourselves become a conversation with God, and this means turning our hopes and fears over to God, entrusting them to God. What this leads to is an inner peace where we fall silent at last in the presence of God, and that inner peace, I take it, is the ultimate answer to prayer. That inner peace is also spiritual enlightenment, moral guidance ("his will is our peace"), and religious assurance.

What is the truth of a life? It is the past, the present, and the future of the life, but it is also, I suppose, one's relation to the past and present and future, for instance fear of the future, especially of death, and regret of the past. To turn the truth of a life into prayer is to do what Dag Hammarskjöld does when he prays at the turning point of his life, "For all that has been—Thanks! To all that shall be—Yes!"[45] What he does is go from regret of the past to "Thanks!" and from fear of the future to "Yes!" It amounts to taking the advice Tolkien has Gandalf give to the king, "To cast aside regret and fear. To do the deed at hand."[46] Here thinking back to the past becomes thanking, and thinking forward to the future is assent that becomes consent.

If I turn the truth of my life into poetry, I come to a symbolic immortality like Goethe's Faust, but if I turn the truth of my life into prayer, I come to eternal life, an *I and thou* relation with the Eternal Thou. I think of the concluding words of Mozart's *Ave Verum,*

Esto nobis praegustatum   Be to us a foretaste
in mortis examine.   in the hour of death.[47]

like the concluding words of the *Ave Maria,* "Pray for us now and at the hour of our death." Faith in eternal life is faith in the survival of the *I and thou* relation with the Eternal Thou, that the *I and thou* with God is eternal. It is in the words of the Gospel of John, "I in them and thou in me."[48]

"The Eternal Feminine draws us on"(*Das Ewigweibliche zieht uns hinan*),[49] the concluding words of Goethe's *Faust,* are an expression of heart's desire, of longing for eternal life. The realization of that longing, though, the realization of heart's desire, is in an *I and thou* with God, as in Saint Augustine's words at the beginning of his *Confessions,* "you have made us for yourself, and our heart is restless until it rests in you."[50] We are made for an *I and thou* with God, and our heart is restless until it rests in an eternal *I and thou.* Saint Augustine's *Confessions* themselves are a sustained prayer, and so are themselves the very realization of the heart's desire that he is envisioning. The human heart rests in God in the inner peace "we all have within us," "a center of stillness surrounded by silence."

"An endless conversation,"[51] that is what Diogenes called Plato's philosophy, and that is how a quest of eternal life begins, in an endless conversation with others, but it becomes an endless conversation with ourselves, and it ends as endless conversation with God. I suppose it is the endlessness of the conversation that points to eternal life. It is true, though, the conversation even with God can come to an end in silence. I think of Pascal saying "The eternal silence of these infinite spaces frightens me" (*Le silence eternel de ces espaces infinis m'effraie*).[52] I think sometimes that I am talking death to death in my endeavor to study all the answers I can find to the question "If I must die someday, what can I do to satisfy my desire to live?" Silence then is an answer, like "the eternal silence of these infinite spaces," though it "frightens me."

Words and music come out of silence and return into silence, and so also the great circle of life and light and love,

> Like a great ring of pure and endless light,
> All calm, as it was bright.

"Where the story-teller is loyal, eternally and unswervingly loyal to the story, there, in the end, silence will speak," Isak Dinesen says. "Where the story has been betrayed, silence is but emptiness."[53] If I am loyal to the story of the great circle of life and light and love, like the Gospel of John, there, in the end, silence will speak, even the eternal silence of these infinite spaces. Words and music come out of silence, even the eternal silence of these infinite spaces, "the words of eternal life," the Word, the one who has "the words of eternal life,"—and the music?—perhaps the Word in the beginning is also the music, "In the beginning is the song."[54] When I am composing music, I have to have silence, I can't be listening to music. Also I have to be at peace.

"It was the word beyond speech."[55] That is the concluding sentence of Hermann Broch's novel *The Death of Virgil*. That, I believe, is what it means to say "in the end, silence will speak." It is as if to say "In the end was the Word," like the Gospel of John saying "In the beginning was the Word." This is the fulfilment, it seems to me, of the quest of eternal life, the answer to the riddle of eternal life. Broch's novel tells the traditional story of Virgil on his deathbed wanting to burn his unfinished *Aeneid*. It is like the story of Saint Thomas Aquinas at the end of his life refusing to finish his *Summa Theologiae,* saying all that he had written seemed to him "like straw."[56] That would make eminent sense if we suppose an encounter at the end with "the word beyond speech," and especially if we suppose that word beyond speech in the end is the same as the Word that is in the beginning.

If I am faithful then to the story of my own life, to my journey with God in time, then I may hope the silence will speak to me in the end, even the eternal silence of these infinite spaces, and it will speak or, rather, somehow communicate "the word beyond speech," and that Word in the end will be the same as the Word in the beginning. It is "the word of life,"[57] as Saint John says in the prologue of his epistle corresponding to the prologue of his gospel, the Word of eternal life, just as Christ in the gospel speaks "the words of eternal life." Silence speaks, I believe, when it is felt as presence, the surrounding silence of "We all have within us a center of stillness surrounded by silence." It is the surrounding silence of the presence of God.

AN ANSWER:
THE ROAD THAT GOES ON

The Road goes ever on and on.
            —J. R. R. Tolkien

So if I must die someday, what can I do to satisfy my desire to live? Take the road in life that goes ever on. There are roads in life that deadend. When Richard Rich seeks "office," Thomas More tells him "Be a teacher."[1] I am tempted to say "office" is a road that deadends but "being a teacher" is a road that goes ever on. Actually, though, what makes a road go ever on is the "wandering joy" of a journey with God in time. When a road lacks the infinity of walking with God, it deadends. And even on a journey with God there is death, as on all human roads, but a death that is full of life. "Enoch walked with God; and he was not, for God took him" (Genesis 5:24).

It is in "the most decisive acts of life," as Reiner Schürmann calls them, speaking of "wandering joy," that we find the road that goes ever on: "in the foundation of a family or of a community, in a dialogue that actualizes 'two words of existence' or again in the acceptance of destiny."[2] It is especially this last, "the acceptance of destiny," that is the decisive act of a life and usually comes from or leads to the other two. Thus when Dag Hammarskjöld at the turning point of his life says "For all that has been—Thanks! To all that shall be—Yes!" he is accepting his destiny and this is indeed the most decisive act of his life. It occurs at the moment when he becomes secretary general of the UN, thus at a kind of founding of a community, and when he enters thereby into a series of dialogues, I suppose you could say, of "two words of existence." The road goes ever on in the perspective of "Thanks!" and "Yes!"—"Thanks!" for the past and "Yes!" to the future, a freedom towards the past and an openness towards the future.

"Yes!" here, to be sure, is Yes to death, and yet there is the infinity here of prayer in "Thanks!" and "Yes!" *The Road Goes Ever On* is the name of Tolkien's song cycle, set to music by Donald Swann.[3] Although God is not mentioned in the song cycle or even in Tolkien's trilogy (except in the appendix as "the One"), I think the infinity of prayer is there and God is there in the sense that things are meant, and there are signs, and the heart speaks, and there is a way. "He used often to say there was only one Road," Frodo says of Bilbo; "that it was like a great river: its springs were at every doorstep, and every path was its tributary."[4] So there is in the song cycle and in the trilogy an image of eternal life in the end, sailing into the West.

There are two images here, The Road Goes Ever On and Sailing into the West. One is of eternal life in life, the other of eternal life in death. It just came to me last night that the music of words is "a tension of essences"[5] that allows the story to come out different ways, happy ending or sad ending, and thus allows the singer of tales to improvise. The Road Goes Ever On is an image that reflects the ongoing tension of essences. Sailing into the West is an image that resolves the tension in a happy ending.

The Road Goes Ever On

"Even the very wise cannot see all ends,"[6] Tolkien has Gandalf say to Frodo, cannot see how a person's life will turn out. What the wise do see, I suppose, is "the tension of essences," the themes at work in a life. I think of the themes in Wagner's *Ring* and I think of the themes I have found in Tolkien's trilogy, things are meant, and there are signs, and the heart speaks, and there is a way. I suppose the Ring itself is another theme, along the lines of Lord Acton's "Power tends to corrupt and absolute power corrupts absolutely."[7] The tension of essences here is especially between good and evil, between the good of things meant and signs and the heart speaking and the way and the evil of power corrupting. The Road goes ever on in this tension until the tension is resolved in the destruction of the Ring and its power, and then it goes on in the tension of good and the aftereffects of evil until all is resolved in sailing into the West.

"'Tension of essences' is close to 'free association,'"[8] Albert Lord says in *The Singer Resumes the Tale.* So it is not just the conflict of good and evil but the free association of theme and theme. The ongoing tension of essences in "The Road goes ever on" is the ongoing association of theme and theme in the story. If I find these same themes in my life story, things are meant and there are signs and the heart speaks and there is a way, I find also the free association of theme and theme. So the way my life story comes out is not simply the same as the story Tolkien is telling. It becomes very true for me that "even the very wise cannot see all ends," and not seeing the end is the essence of the road going ever on. "Our life has no end in just the way in which our visual field has no limits,"[9] Wittgenstein says. It is a matter of not seeing the end.

It is true, Wittgenstein says "Death is not an event of life: we do not live to experience death" (or in C. K. Ogden's translation, "Death is not an event of life. Death is not lived through")[10] and that is why he says in the same place "Our life has no end in just the way in which our visual field has no limits." I want to say, on the contrary, that death *is* an event of life and we do live to experience death (or death is lived through). So when I say our life is endless in that we do not see the end, I mean we do not foresee the end. We come to the end, nevertheless, and go through death to life, and so again the road goes ever on. Wittgenstein also says in the same place "eternal life belongs to those who live in the present," but I want to say *eternal life belongs to those who live in the presence, to those who live in the infinity of prayer.*

What I mean by "the infinity of prayer" is an *I and thou* relation with the infinite Thou. "The Road Goes Ever On," Tolkien's song, though it is not cast into the form of prayer, has the virtue of a prayer like Newman's "Lead, Kindly Light, Lead Thou me on." In Tolkien's song one is led by the Road; in Newman's one is led by the Kindly Light. Tolkien's Road, I believe, is like *The Road Past the View* of Georgia O'Keefe's painting. It leads one into the unknown. It is also like "The Road Not Taken" of Robert Frost's poem, for if there is only one Road, as Tolkien says, then the Road Not Taken rejoins the Road Taken in life.

Here is the "free association" evoked by the "tension of essences," The Road Goes Ever On and Lead, Kindly Light and The Road Past the View and The Road Not Taken. Tolkien's own associations appear in his description, "He used to say there was only one Road: that it was like a great river: its springs were at every doorstep, and every path was its tributary." But what of roads in life that deadend? There are roads in life that are leading nowhere, lacking possibilities for advance, progress, or further action. We speak, for instance, of a deadend job, a deadend policy, a human relationship that is going nowhere. All these roads that deadend, do they deadend in the road that goes ever on? I suppose this is what it means to say "there was only one Road: that it was like a great river: its springs were at every doorstep, and every path was its tributary." So even a deadend job, a deadend policy, a relationship that is going nowhere, deadends in the road that goes ever on.

There is a parable of the road that deadends and the road that goes ever on in the Russian short novel, *The Yellow Arrow* by Victor Pelevin. The main character Andrei is on the road that deadends in the train called The Yellow Arrow, but he manages to get off when the train stops (and time stops),

> He turned and walked away, not really thinking about where he was going. Soon he found himself walking on an asphalt road across an open meadow, and a band of bright sky appeared on the horizon. The rumbling of the wheels behind his back gradually faded, and soon he could hear quite clearly sounds he'd never heard before—a dry chirping on the grass, the sighing of the wind and his own quiet steps.[11]

That is the concluding paragraph. He is on the road that goes ever on and he has gotten off the road that deadends. Or if you will, the road that deadends has deadended for him in the road that goes ever on.

What then is the road that deadends, and what is the road that goes ever on? The Yellow Arrow stops when time stops. That is the key, I think. In the preface to *Being and Time* Heidegger says time is "the possible horizon for any understanding whatsoever of Being," and then in the body of the work he describes human existence as essentially "Being toward death."[12] I suppose the road that goes ever on, by contrast, means Being toward life, living toward life, living toward eternal life, and so, I gather, it means turning time's arrow into love's direction. And what is love's direction? "The love is from God and of God and toward God," as the old man of the desert said to Lawrence of Arabia. The Yellow Arrow in Victor Pelevin's story is time's arrow, I suppose, the arrow that goes from past to future. Love's direction is from God and to God.

Now let us look more closely at "Being toward death." The Yellow Arrow in the story is traveling toward a wrecked bridge, toward death, I suppose, and it is said one cannot get off the train, though Andrei does manage to get off when the train stops and time stops. "The philosopher does not believe," Heidegger says in *The Concept of Time*. "If the philosopher asks about time, then he has resolved to understand time in terms of time,"[13] and not in terms of eternity. So time is opaque for him, not transparent to or even translucent with eternity. That is like the idea that it is impossible to get off the Yellow Arrow. Yet Andrei manages to do it when the train stops and time stops. If time then is "a changing image of eternity,"[14] as Plato says, and is transparent to eternity or translucent with eternity, it is possible to go from "Being toward death" to Being toward life, living toward life, toward eternal life.

It is all a matter of orientation, of direction in life. If "the unconscious is the direction we are not looking,"[15] as Alfred Adler says, then going from death to life is a matter of looking in the direction we have not been looking. And if "love is a direction,"[16] as Simone Weil says, it is a matter of looking in love's direction, "from God and of God and towards God." Death, from this point of view, is an event of life like birth rather than simple nonexistence. There is a combination here of willingness and hope, willingness to die and yet hope to live, like the combination of willingness to walk alone and yet hope of companionship in life. By itself the willingness is what Kierkegaard calls "infinite resignation," but the paradoxical combination of willingness and hope is what he calls "faith." So the orientation of faith in eternal life means looking in the direction of eternal life, a direction we have not been looking in our infinite resignation to death. So too the orientation of faith is toward *I and thou*, whereas infinite resignation to the loneliness of the human condition is simply willingness to walk alone. That willingness is still there in faith, but it is combined with an openness to the mystery of *I and thou*.

Here again we come to the "tension of essences" that is close to "free association." "Do not seek death. Death will find you," Dag Hammarskjöld writes in *Markings*. "But seek the road which makes death a fulfilment."[17] For me the road that makes death a fulfilment is "the road of the union of love with God,"[18] as Saint John of the Cross names it in the preface to his *Dark Night of the Soul*. To me life is about learning to love, learning to love "with all your heart, and with all your soul, and with all your might," as is said in the Torah, and "with all your mind," as is added in the Gospels.[19] So the road that goes ever on, the road that makes death a fulfilment, is the mystic road of love, "the road of the union of love with God." For if you love with all your mind, and with all your heart, and with all your soul, and with all your might, I can see, it is God you love.

If the love of God is simply joy at the thought of God, as Spinoza says—for me joy at the thought of being on a journey with God in time—then the love of God is the "wandering joy" that Meister Eckhart speaks of, the joy of being on a journey with God. The difficult thing about learning to love, according to this, is the element of detachment in love, the detachment in "wandering joy." One who is detached, heart-free I would say, "experiences such a joy that no one would be able to tear it away." But such a one "remains unsettled." One who has let oneself be and who has let God be "lives in a wandering joy, or joy without a cause."[20] The difficult thing is letting be (*Gelassenheit*), letting others be, letting oneself be, letting God be, the element of detachment in love. But if I can learn letting be and openness to the mystery, I can live in wandering joy.

Living in wandering joy, I am walking on "the road of the union of love with God" where the union of love with God is, as Saint Teresa of Avila says, "a union of wills,"[21] a union of the human will and the divine will. But how is a human being to know what the will of God is? Dante's saying is the criterion, I take it, "his will is our peace" (*la sua voluntate e nostra pace*): the criterion of the union of wills is the sense of inner peace. I know I am on the road of the union of love with God, according to this, when I am living in the peace. But since it is a union of wills, it is a union of direction, and it is a road, and indeed a road that goes ever on. I am walking with God on a road that does not deadend. All the same, I have to die someday, hoping what was true of Enoch will be true of me, "Enoch walked with God; and he was not, for God took him."

If the music of words is "a tension of essences" that allows the story to come out in different ways, happy ending and sad ending, walking with God is living at peace in the tension of essences, and thus is *a rest in restlessness*[22] that becomes a repose in God, as in the biblical imperative "Seek peace, and ensue it." The tension of essences by itself reflects the restlessness of desire that moves constantly from image to image of fulfilment. How then can we ever come to rest in this perpetual motion unless it is possible somehow to rest in the motion itself like a whirling gyroscope poised on a point? It is possible to do this by accepting the perpetual motion of our imagination reflecting the perpetual motion of desire. A willing restlessness becomes a rest, a repose in restless movement. And it becomes a rest in our "center of stillness surrounded by silence" that Dag Hammarskjöld speaks of in his brochure for the Meditation Room at the UN, "We all have within us a center of stillness surrounded by silence," the still point.

"Song is the leap of mind in the eternal breaking out into sound,"[23] Saint Thomas Aquinas says in the preface to his commentary on the Psalms. If I say then that the music of words is "a tension of essences," song is a breaking of the tension. Consider the short song Beethoven places before the last movement of his last string quartet:

Grave	Muss es sein?	Must it be?
Allegro	Es muss sein!	It must be!
	Es muss sein!	It must be![24]

I know the story of money owed and Beethoven writing a lighthearted canon on these words, a canon which we have, but I take it that the question and answer have become serious in the last movement of the last quartet, and that Beethoven goes from *Grave* to *Allegro* as from gravity to grace, from infinite resignation to faith. His last string quartet ends with words just as his last symphony ends with words (an ode to joy), and it is a happy ending.

Song is a breaking of the tension of essences just as love is "the breaking of the tension between the self and the other," as Gabriel Marcel says, "the subordination of the self to a superior reality, a reality at my deepest level, more truly me than I am myself."[25] The deeper reality in song is the eternal. "Song [*canticum*] is the leap of mind" (*exultatio mentis*), the exultation of mind, "in the eternal" (*de aeternis habita*), about eternal things, "breaking out into sound" (*prorumpens in vocem*), breaking out into voice. Saint Thomas is thinking of the Psalms here, and so the deeper reality is clearly the eternal. If we speak not only of sacred song but also of secular song, we can still say this insofar as time is "a changing image of eternity," but the eternal, the deeper reality, is more hidden behind its changing image, time. The deeper reality in love is the deeper self, "a center of stillness surrounded by silence" where God dwells in the heart. Song is God in the heart singing out to God in the universe.

So when I say time is "a changing image of eternity," I am saying the stages of my life, childhood, youth, manhood, and age, are a changing image of God in me or of God in my heart, just as the world in time is a changing image of God in the universe. The eternal itself is God in the heart (Atman) and God in the universe (Brahman), and God dwelling in the heart and God dwelling in the universe, according to the Upanishads, are one and the same.

Love's road, therefore, "the road of the union of love with God," goes ever on and on, for God in the heart and God in the universe are one and the same, and so love's road is "the road which makes death a fulfilment," the road which makes death a going to the heart of the universe. Thus death is not a going out of existence so much as a going to the heart of existence. If "we all have within us a center of stillness surrounded by silence," God's presence, as I have been saying, is the silence surrounding our center of stillness, whereas the center itself is the deep self, "the eternal self,"[26] as Kierkegaard calls it. The "union of love with God" is our *I and thou* relation with God. Love's road is the road of our journey with God in time, and love itself is the "wandering joy" of our journey. It is our joy at the thought of God being with us on the way.

Love's road going ever on is a guiding image, "a light when all other lights go out,"[27] as Tolkien says, for what such a light shows is hope where it seems there is no hope. "If one does not hope, one will not find the unhoped-for," Heraclitus says, "since there is no trail leading to it and no path."[28] Love's road going ever on means there is a way even when it seems there is no way, there is hope even when it seems there is no hope, and so if one hopes one will find the unhoped-for, one will find a way. There is a distinction between hope as *espoir* and hope as *esperance,* Jean Giono says,[29] between hope set upon an object and hope open to the unhoped-for. The one kind of hope is a road that deadends, the other a road that goes ever on.

"There is no trail leading to it, and no path," as Heraclitus says, unless hope itself is the trail, unless hope itself is the path leading to the unhoped-for, hope as *esperance,* open to the unhoped for. Thus at the end Frodo sings

> Still round the corner there may wait
> A new road or a secret gate;
> And though I oft have passed them by,
> A day will come at last when I
> Shall take the hidden paths that run
> West of the Moon, East of the Sun.[30]

If the music of words is a tension of essences that allows the story to come out in different ways, happy ending and sad ending, and thus allows the singer of tales to improvise, hope leading to the unhoped-for allows for the surprise ending. "'Where are you going, Master?' cried Sam, though at last he understood what was happening. 'To the Havens, Sam,' said Frodo."[31] The ending is a surprise to Sam, though it is the outcome of hope leading to the unhoped-for, a new road, a secret gate, the hidden paths that run West of the Moon, East of the Sun. It is like "the angel's cry" that Michel Poizat speaks of that takes us "beyond the pleasure principle in opera,"[32] beyond expected pleasure to unexpected joy.

Sailing into the West

"Does the flap of a butterfly's wings in Brazil set off a tornado in Texas?"[33] That is the question, asked by Edward Lorenz, that was the beginning of our present-day *chaos theory.* Something similar could be asked about "the tension of essences" we have been speaking of in story and in song. Could a very slight difference in the tension of essences lead to a sad ending instead of a happy ending? Tolkien has a poem called "The Sea-bell" or "Frodo's Dream" (spelled "Frodos Dreme") where he imagines a sad ending instead of the happy ending of Frodo's story in *The*

Lord of the Rings, sailing into the West. He says "the title shows that it was associated with the dark and despairing dreams which visited him in March and October during his last three years."[34] According to this poem, Frodo goes sailing into the West, only to find it empty and deserted, though he cries out "Answer my call! Come forth all! Speak to me words! Show me a face!"[35] And he is forced to go back home, defeated and despairing.

On the other hand, he has a dream in the house of Tom Bombadil, and "either in his dreams or out of them, he could not tell which," he "heard a sweet singing running in his mind: a song that seemed to come like a pale light behind a grey rain-curtain, and growing stronger to turn the veil all to glass and silver, until at last it was rolled back, and a far green country opened before him under a swift sunrise."[36] And that is the dream that comes true. I think of the two portals in the *Aeneid*, the gate of ivory where false dreams and visions come and the gate of horn where true dreams and visions come to us:

> Twofold the portals of sleep,
> and twofold 'tis said in their nature;
> one of them fashioned from horn
> releases the true visions skyward;
> carven from elephants' tusks
> the other is gleaming and candid,
> through this, however, the spirits
> are sending up false apparitions.[37]

What is "the butterfly effect" here? What is the tension of essences, I mean, that can make the one dream or the other come true? Is it something like Beethoven's short song?

> *Grave*　Must it be?
> *Allegro*　It must be!
> 　　　　It must be!

where "Must it be?" expresses infinite resignation, willingness without hope, and thus the despairing dream, and "It must be! It must be!" expresses faith, willingness and hope, and thus the dream of eternal life. What must be? Death and yet life, aloneness and yet companionship. The willingness to die, I mean, and yet the hope to live, the willingness to walk alone and yet the hope to be unalone. If it were simply death and aloneness, that would be the despairing dream. If it is death and yet life, aloneness and yet companionship, that is the dream of eternal life. The one encompasses the other, "It must be!" encompasses "Must it be?"—faith encompasses infinite resignation, willingness and hope encompass bare willingness.

　　If we go from infinite resignation to faith, we make the move that is made in the song and the story. These are Kierkegaard's terms in *Fear and Trembling.* As I have it here, his "knight of infinite resignation" sings *Grave* "Must it be?" and his "knight of faith" then sings *Allegro* "It must be! It must be!" In the story, too, as Tolkien tells it, Frodo goes from the *Grave* of "the dark and despairing dreams which visited him in March and October during his last three years" to the *Allegro* of his sailing into the West at the end.

　　"Infinite resignation expresses the recognition and acceptance of God's love. But faith is man's finite repetition of God's love for him."[38] That is how Barbara Anderson interprets Kierkegaard's terms. The *Grave* "Must it be?" according to this, would mean "Must I be who I am?" To recognize and accept who I am is to recognize and accept

God's love for me in creating me. The *Allegro* "It must be! It must be!" then would be my finite repetition of God's love for me. By relating to myself and willing to be myself, Kierkegaard says, I am "grounded transparently" in God.[39] My infinite resignation would encompass my willingness to die and my willingness to walk alone in my willingness to be myself. My faith would encompass that willingness along with my hope to live and my hope of companionship. My hope would be ultimately in God's love, in the wonder of my existence, "the mystical" as Wittgenstein calls it, that I am though I will die.

"Not *how* the world is, is the mystical, but *that* it is," he says, and "The feeling of the world as a limited whole is the mystical feeling" and "There is indeed the inexpressible. This *shows* itself; it is the mystical."[40] Recognition of God's love, I gather, is recognition of the mystical. I am, though I am only one of countless human beings who live and have lived, and so I am loved. "Why did it come to me? Why was I chosen?"[41] Frodo asks, speaking of the Ring, but I could ask the same thing, speaking of existence, "Why did it come to me? Why was I chosen?" And that is the force of the *Grave* "Must it be?" in the song. "Such questions cannot be answered," Gandalf replies to Frodo, or they cannot be answered except with the *Allegro* "It must be! It must be!" For it is not *how* I am that is mystical but *that* I am.

It is "infinite resignation" to say *Yes* to God's love, and yet "The feeling of the world as a limited whole is the mystical feeling." For my *Yes* encompasses my willingness to die and my willingness to walk alone in my willingness to be myself. It is a *Yes* to infinite love but a *Yes* that accepts my own limits. So if I ask of my existence "Why did it come to me? Why was I chosen?" Gandalf's reply to Frodo is good for me too, "Such questions cannot be answered . . . You may be sure that it was not for any merit that others do not possess: not for power or wisdom, at any rate. But you have been chosen, and you must therefore use such strength and heart and wits as you have."

It is possible, though, to recognize and accept one's calling and yet to do so without hope. That is truly "infinite resignation" and not yet "faith." When Frodo and Sam are in Mordor, on the way to fulfilling their mission of destroying the Ring of Power, Sam tries to rekindle Frodo's hope, but does not succeed.

> "What did I tell you? Something's happening!" cried Sam . . . "Things are looking up, Mr. Frodo. Haven't you got some hope now?"
>
> "Well, no, not much, Sam," Frodo sighed. "That's away beyond the mountains. We're going east not west. And I'm so tired. And the Ring is so heavy, Sam. And I begin to see it in my mind all the time, like a great wheel of fire."[42]

"There is indeed the inexpressible," as Wittgenstein says. "This *shows* itself; it is the mystical." This is how hope arises where there was no hope. Eternal life is like this, it *shows* itself. Staying within the limits of the expressible, Wittgenstein says "If by eternity is understood not endless temporal duration but timelessness, then he lives eternally who lives in the present," or in another translation, "eternal life belongs to those who live in the present."[43] But if we move on to what he considers the inexpressible, we should say *eternal life belongs to those who live in the presence.* "This *shows* itself," as he says; "it is the mystical." It shows itself in Beethoven's short song (at least as I am interpreting it) when he sings "It must be! It must be!" It shows itself in Tolkien's story in sailing into the West. Eternal life in the song must be! must be! And it belongs in the story to those who sail into the West. If it were merely a matter of living in the present (as in the self-help books), it would not be worth a story or a song. But if it is a matter of living in the presence, it is indeed the matter of story and song.

There is hope in the *Allegro* of the song, according to my interpretation, willingness and hope. "To *choose* necessity," Helen Luke says, "is a very different thing from acquiescing with resentment or with hopeless resignation to the inevitable."[44] So I take it that the words "It must be! It must be!" express a choosing of necessity, a willingness and yet a hope, a willingness to die and yet a hope to live, a willingness to walk alone and yet a hope of companionship. If my willingness is a Yes to God's love, then my hope is in God's love, and that kind of hope is open to the unknown, to the unhoped-for. As the High One says in Patricia McKillip's *Riddle-Master,* "Beyond logic, beyond reason, beyond hope. Trust me."[45]

There is hope also in Tolkien's story. "If your hurts grieve you still and the memory of your burden is heavy," Arwen tells Frodo, "then you may pass into the West, until all your wounds and weariness are healed," and Elrond tells him, "For about this time of year, when the leaves are gold before they fall, look for Bilbo in the woods of the Shire. I shall be with him."[46] So he has the promise of sailing into the West, and not alone, until all his wounds and weariness are healed. He did not have this promise in the beginning, except in the form of a dream, but only after his mission was accomplished. Then too he had those nightmares of despair, and at those times he held on to a white stone

Arwen had given him to wear and to remind him of the promise and of hope.

Sailing into the West is an image of death and passing to Frodo's friends who witness it, Sam and Merry and Pippin. "But to Sam the evening deepened to darkness as he stood at the Haven; and as he looked at the grey sea he saw only a shadow on the waters that was soon lost in the West." But to Frodo himself and his companions on the ship, sailing into the West is an image of eternal life. "And the ship went out into the High Sea and passed on into the West, until at last on a night of rain Frodo smelled a sweet fragrance on the air and heard the sound of singing that came over the water. And then it seemed to him as in his dream in the house of Bombadil, the grey rain-curtain turned all to silver glass and was rolled back, and he beheld white shores and beyond them a far green country under a swift sunrise."[47] Death is like that, I gather, a passing to us who witness it but eternal life to those who go through it to the other side.

It is true, Tolkien makes a distinction between immortality *within* the circles of the world and eternal life *beyond* the circles of the world. When Aragorn dies (according to the story Tolkien tells in the Appendix), he tells Arwen, "In sorrow we must go, but not in despair. Behold! we are not bound forever to the circles of the world, and beyond them is more than memory. Farewell!"[48] A similar idea occurs earlier in the story of Beren and Luthien. "But she chose mortality, and to die from the world, so that she might follow him," Aragorn tells the hobbits, "and it is sung that they met again beyond the Sundering Seas, and after a brief time walking alive once more in the green woods, together they passed, long ago, beyond the confines of this world."[49]

To speak of "the circles of the world, and beyond them" or "beyond the confines of this world" is to speak of the world as a limited whole, as Wittgenstein says. "The contemplation of the world *sub specie aeterni* is its contemplation as a limited whole," he says, and "The feeling of the world as a limited whole is the mystical feeling."[50] Sailing into the West too in Tolkien's imagery is leaving the confines of Middle-earth. "They are sailing, sailing, sailing over the Sea, they are going into the West and leaving us," as Sam says, "half chanting the words."[51] I think, by comparison, of present-day cosmological thinking. If we think in that way, and I have done some such thinking myself, we are contemplating the world sub specie aeterni, contemplating it as a limited whole, and our feeling of the world as a limited whole is the mystical feeling.

"Did you mean this world? Or is there another?"
"There are two of them and I tell you there is only one of them and it is enough."[52]

That is a dialogue that occurs in Paul Claudel's *Tidings Brought to Mary*. It makes sense to me, seeing the world in terms of the great circle of life and light and love. It is as Rilke says in one of his letters, "The true pattern of life extends through both domains, the blood with the greatest circuit runs through both: there is neither a This-side nor a That-side but a single great unity in which the beings who transcend us, the angels, have their habitation."[53] There is this world and the other world if you consider the two sides of the circulation of the blood, the arteries carrying the blood from the heart, the life and light and love coming from God, and the veins carrying the blood back to the heart, the return of life and light and love to God. But there is only one world and it is enough if you consider the unity of the great circle itself.

I know of the "many worlds interpretation" of quantum mechanics that goes with the idea of "the wave function of the universe"[54] where alternative paths make alternative worlds. I want to go instead with Tolkien's image of one Road where the road not taken rejoins the road taken. "He used often to say there was only one Road; that it was like a great river: its springs were at every doorstep, and every path was its tributary."[55] I wonder if "the path integral" approach to quantum mechanics could be given this kind of interpretation. At any rate it seems to be true of the paths of life that the road not taken rejoins or can rejoin the road taken. How this comes about, it is true, is not always as simple as it has been for me, where the way of music, my road not taken in life, has rejoined the way of words, my road taken in life.

So I speak now of "the music of words" and say it is "a tension of essences" that allows the story to come out different ways, happy ending or sad ending, and thus allows the singer of tales to improvise. I was not expecting to give such significance to improvisation, but the idea of "a tension of essences" leads that way. The relation of words and music is looser than I expected, speaking of "the music of words." In a tone language like Chinese or even Norwegian it could be tighter, but in English or in German it seems to be simply a matter of mapping music on words and mapping words on music. Words and music seem to correspond to the two hemispheres of the brain, words to the left brain and the right hand, music to the right brain and the left hand. So the rejoining of the ways I am envisioning seems to be a matter of human wholeness.

If I take a "path integral" approach to the paths of life, I would not have to take all possible paths like Lord Ronald who "flung himself upon his horse and rode madly off in all directions."[56] Instead I would take the path of wholeness, learning to love "with all your heart, and with all your soul, and with all your might" and as the Gospels add, "with all your mind." That would be the one Road, like a great river, its springs at every doorstep, every path its tributary. That would be the road taken that the road not taken rejoins. If it were the way of words, my road taken in life, then the way of music, my road not taken, would rejoin it in learning to love with all my might, like David who "danced before the Lord with all his might." Yet how can the way of words be a way of learning to love? By turning the truth of the life into prayer, I suppose, like Saint Augustine, just as Goethe turned the truth of his life into poetry. Thus prayer can become the prayer of mind, the prayer of heart, and finally the prayer of soul.

If I learn to love, like Saint Augustine, by learning to pray, I can start with the prayer of mind, like his in the *Soliloquies,* "May I know me! May I know thee!" And I can go on to the prayer of heart, like his in the *Confessions,* "Our heart is restless until it rests in thee." And I can come to the prayer of soul, like his in the *City of God,*

> These goods are good because you are,
> And nothing ours is in them but our sin
> Of loving them by you instead of you.[57]

an evening song to be sung at the lighting of the candle, all we have left of his poetry, and it is of words set to music. I think of it as prayer of soul because it expresses detachment in love, the difficulty of loving with all your soul, but as it goes over into music it goes over into loving with all your might. Or I can go from learning to pray the Psalms as he does in the *Confessions* to setting the Psalms to music, as Stravinsky does in his *Symphony of Psalms.* I can go, that is, from words to music.

There is indeed one Road then, as Tolkien says, and it is the path of wholeness, of learning to love with all your mind and heart and soul, and when words are set to music, with all your might; and it is like a great river, its springs at every doorstep, every path its tributary.

A SPIRITUAL JOURNEY

> He used often to say there was only one Road; that it
> was like a great river: its springs were at every doorstep,
> and every path was its tributary.
>
> —J. R. R. Tolkien

"I began to have an idea of my life," Joanna Field writes, "not as the slow shaping of achievement to fit my preconceived purposes, but as the gradual discovery and growth of a purpose I did not know."[1] That purpose for me is learning to love, the path of wholeness, learning to love with all your mind and with all your heart and with all your soul and with all your might. To me that is the one Road that Tolkien speaks of, the Road Taken that is rejoined by the Road Not Taken.

I want to take then a *path integral* approach to the paths of life, borrowing the term from quantum mechanics but leaving out its mathematical aspect and taking it just as a metaphor for the one Road that Tolkien speaks of, the Road that goes ever on, like a great river, its springs at every doorstep, every path its tributary. The mathematical aspect of the path integral is the *sum over histories*, as it is called, where all possible trajectories are added together. This would not work for the paths of life, for as Robert Frost says in his poem "The Road Not Taken":

> . . . I could not travel both
> And be one traveler . . .[2]

I could not travel both the road taken and the road not taken, he is saying, and be one traveler. All the same, I have found the road taken in my life, the way of words, can *rejoin* the road not taken, the way of music, and that rejoining of the ways, I believe, is what constitutes Tolkien's one Road, and is what I want to call the path integral approach to the paths of life.

"We imagine divine grace to be finite. For this reason we tremble . . ." it is said in Isak Dinesen's story "Babette's Feast." "We tremble before making our choice in life, and after having made it again tremble in fear of having chosen wrong. But the moment comes when our eyes are opened, and we see and realize that grace is infinite." And this infinity of grace, as I understand it, means our road not taken rejoins our road taken. "See! that which we have chosen is given us, and that which we have refused is, also and at the same time, granted us. Ay, that which we have rejected is poured upon us abundantly."[3] Certainly, that has been true for me, the way of music, my road not taken, rejoining in these later years the way of words, my road taken. How this may happen more generally, though, is shrouded in some mystery. Let us see if we can penetrate this mystery.

What of roads of love not taken? What of unrequited love? I expect it is all a matter of wholeness, that the one Road is that of wholeness, learning to love with all your mind and heart and soul, as I was learning on my way of words, and learning to love with all your might, like David who "danced before the Lord with all his might," meant returning to the way of music, my road not taken. So it is, I am guessing, with other lives, the road taken leads on by way of wholeness to the road not taken.

The Road Taken

When we take a road in life, it is not usually with the idea of learning to love but of following someone else we love and admire. "He did not tell Gandalf, but as he was speaking a great desire to follow Bilbo flamed up in his heart—to follow Bilbo, and even perhaps to find him again," Tolkien says of Frodo at the beginning of his adventure. "It was so strong that it overcame his fear: he could almost have run out there and then down the road without his hat, as Bilbo had done on a similar morning long ago."[4] We start with "mimetic desire," as René Girard calls it, and only come in the end to what I call "heart's desire." It is true, Girard argues that all desire is mimetic. We see what others desire and we desire what they desire. But I think we come at last to heart's desire, what we truly want, as Tolstoy did in his late years when he wrote in his journal "God is my desire."

"In his diary which he gave me to read, I was struck by a strange aphorism: *God is my desire*," Max Gorky writes of Tolstoy. "Today, on returning him the book, I asked what it meant. An unfinished thought, he said, glancing at the page and screwing up his eyes. I must have wanted to say: 'God is my desire to know Him . . . No, not that . . .' He began to laugh, and, rolling up the book into a tube, he put it into the big pocket of his blouse. With God he has very suspicious relations; they sometimes remind me of the relation of two bears in one den."[5]

Coming to the heart's desire, I gather, can be a long process and can seem obscure to one who has not gone through it. There is a saying of Confucius describing the stages: "He said at fifteen I wanted to learn, at thirty I had a foundation, at forty, a certitude, at fifty, knew the orders of heaven, at sixty was ready to listen to them, at seventy could follow my own heart's desire without overstepping the t-square."[6] What is it to know the orders of heaven? What is it to listen to them? And what is it to follow your own heart's desire without overstepping the t-square? This is Ezra Pound's translation of Confucius that I am using. I take it the orders of heaven are the mandates of heaven, what we would call the will of God, and as Dante said "his will is our peace," and that is how we know it, and that is how we follow our heart's desire without overstepping the t-square, by living in the peace.

Once in a conversation with René Girard I proposed to him my idea of heart's desire as distinct from mimetic desire. "That sounds to me like peace, not desire," he replied. And that indeed is how I envision heart's desire, as inner peace, but I see that as something to be desired, to be sought as in the biblical imperative, "Seek peace, and ensue it."[7] We begin with mimetic desire, I believe, but we end with heart's desire, seeking peace and ensuing it. We can go through stages, like those of Confucius, wanting to learn, finding a foundation, a certitude, seeking the will of God, and seeking its peace.

"Desire is always reflection on desire,"[8] René Girard says, meaning we are always miming the desires of others. I wonder if that is why we find it so difficult to endure happiness. I think of the stories, of the Garden of Eden, of

Lost Horizon, where we seem unable to stay in paradise. What draws us out seems to be some kind of mimetic desire, "your eyes shall be opened, and ye shall be as gods, knowing good and evil."⁹ Frodo is happy, living in the Shire, but he is drawn to follow Bilbo into adventure, into the unknown, although he feels regret. "When the light of the last farm was far behind, peeping among the trees, Frodo turned and waved a hand in farewell. 'I wonder if I shall ever look down into that valley again,' he said quietly," and Sam too, as "his old life lay behind in the mists" and "dark adventure lay in front," felt regret and "for a moment had a passing wish that Mr. Frodo could have gone on living quietly at Bag End."¹⁰

My own experience of mimetic desire took the form of spiritual ambition, reading lives of saints, especially Chesterton's of Saint Francis being in love with God and of Saint Thomas Aquinas answering the divine offer "Ask what I shall give you" with "Nothing, Lord, but you yourself," and this spiritual ambition led me to the religious life and the priesthood. Then came that choice between the way of words and the way of music, and my choice was the way of words, the right choice for me, I think in retrospect, for words, going with my left brain and my right hand, were my stronger side, and music, going with my right brain and my left hand, was my weaker side, though music was there in my life from the beginning (I used to pick out melodies on the piano when I was three years old).

But it is the encounter with death, I believe, coming to a vivid awareness of our mortality, that carries us from mimetic to heart's desire. Thus for me, around the age of thirty, I was writing my first book, *The City of the Gods*, and I came to that question, "If I must die someday, what can I do to satisfy my desire to live?" The heart's desire makes its appearance here as "the desire to live," but that desire, as I saw it and felt it, turns out to be a desire for eternal life. I see this encounter with death also in Tolkien's trilogy when Frodo, on his way to Rivendell and reunion with Bilbo, the fulfilment of his mimetic desire, meets the Barrow Wights and then the Black Riders and has a near-death experience that changes his whole sensibility. This is the thing, I believe, that sets him on the road of the heart's desire.

In the saying of Confucius about the stages on life's way it is in the last three stages that the heart's desire emerges, "at fifty, knew the orders of heaven, at sixty was ready to listen to them, at seventy could follow my own heart's desire without overstepping the t-square." In Tolkien's story too there is something like knowing the orders of heaven and listening to them. "A great dread fell on him, as if he was awaiting the pronouncement of some doom that he had long foreseen and vainly hoped might after all never be spoken," Tolkien says of Frodo at the Council of Elrond. "An overwhelming longing to rest and remain at peace by Bilbo's side filled all his heart. At last with an effort he spoke, and wondered to hear his own words, as if some other will was using his small voice. I will take the Ring, he said, though I do not know the way."[11]

It is not until his mission is accomplished that he feels the peace I have been associating with the heart's desire. "In his eyes there was peace now, neither strain of will, nor madness, nor any fear. His burden was taken away."[12] Before that point peace seemed to go rather with his mimetic desire, "An overwhelming longing to rest and remain at peace by Bilbo's side filled all his heart." Perhaps then the stages that Confucius speaks of are essential, before being able to follow the heart's desire I have to know the orders of heaven and I have to be ready to listen to them. That would better explain the call of prophets, especially that of reluctant prophets, and the experience of conversion, especially that of reluctant converts. Although "his will is our peace," as Dante says, coming to know the will and coming to listen to the will can come before the peace.

So then to go back to first principles, "The great learning takes root in clarifying the way wherein intelligence increases through the process of looking straight into one's own heart and acting on the results," according to Confucius; "it is rooted in watching with affection the way people grow; it is rooted in coming to rest, being at ease in perfect equity."[13] The first of these three principles, about looking straight into one's own heart and acting on the results, is what I call following the heart's desire. The second, about watching with affection the way people grow, is what I call studying the stages on life's way. And the third, about coming to rest in perfect equity, is what I call coming to inner peace.

These three principles make it possible to discover one's way in life instead of arbitrarily choosing it. By looking into my own heart, watching the way other people grow, and coming to inner peace, I find my way. When I first started teaching, I had read Jean Paul Sartre and had taken up his idea that we simply choose our way and thus choose our own essence, but the experience of teaching and learning from the young people I was teaching and also that of reading Tolkien and seeing how his characters always wait for the heart to speak before choosing ("My heart speaks clearly at last")[14] led me to believe we discover our way in life rather than arbitrarily choosing it.

There is a mimetic element here still, though, René Girard would be quick to point out, "watching with affection the way people grow." As I see it, there is a double movement here, passing over to other people and coming back again to oneself. You can see this process in the studies artists and composers do in preparation for their own work. I think of Stravinsky orchestrating all the piano sonatas of Beethoven. These were studies in preparation for his original work in composing his own ballets, the *Firebird*, *Petroushka*, and the *Rite of Spring*. If I pass over to others thus and watch with affection the way they grow, I come back again to my own life with new insight. So mimetic desire leads back into heart's desire.

"Our heart is restless until it rests in you," Saint Augustine's principle, seems to contain and explain all three of Confucius' principles, from following the heart to coming to rest, and the way people go from the one to the other. The restless movement of desire and imagination, going from one thing to another, is stilled in our center of stillness surrounded by silence, and the surrounding silence can be interpreted, I have been saying, as the presence of God. So the road we take in life, if we are discovering our way and not just arbitrarily choosing it, will be the road where our restless heart comes to rest in God, and this rest will be on the way, I am thinking, not just at the end of the road. It will mean living in our center of stillness surrounded by the silence of God's presence, living in it and moving with it, like staying in the quiet eye of a moving storm.

What then of the Road Not Taken? I expect to find it on the Road Taken, living in the center of stillness surrounded by the divine silence, moving with the quiet eye of the storm. If the Road Taken is that of learning to love, and that for me is the way of words, the Road Not Taken will be learning to love "with all your might," when the way of words leads into the way of music, of song and dance. That is the way it is for me in terms of words and music, but how to put this more generally? If the dimensions of life I have been living in are the stronger ones for me, taking the Road Not Taken will mean entering into the weaker dimensions. If I have been living in the mind, it will mean living in the heart, or then again living in the soul, or then again living in the body.

So then the more general formula is that of Deuteronomy, to love "with all your heart, and with all your soul, and with all your might," adding from the Gospels "with all your mind," and the Road Taken will be those dimensions in which you live, as for instance C. S. Lewis in *Shadowlands*[15] living in his mind and in his soul and his wife Joy living in her heart. The Road Not Taken will then be the dimensions in which you have to learn to live, C. S. Lewis learning to live in the heart, Joy learning to live in the soul. What is still missing in this example is learning to live in the body, to love "with all your might," as in Pope John Paul II on *The Theology of the Body*.[16] Or as I see it, learning to live in the musical dimension, as in "David danced before the Lord with all his might."

If the Road Not Taken then for me is "the path taken by the soul of the dancer"[17] as Kleist calls it, the Road Taken leads into it when the way of words becomes for me the way of song, "the leap of mind in the eternal breaking out into sound,"[18] as song leads into dance. How again am I to put this more generally? I suppose by saying the life of the spirit, mind and heart and soul, must become incarnate in the flesh, and thus you learn to love "with all your might." For me, nevertheless, this will mean finding where the path of song leads into "the path taken by the soul of the dancer." First, though, I must discover where the way of words leads into the way of song. If, as Vico believed, "the world's first languages were in song,"[19] my going from words to song will be a going back to the beginning.

For myself that transition from words to song came with my book *Love's Mind* (1993), the two song cycles at the end, Ayasofya and Songs about Songs. That was my return to music, but music united with words, what I have come to call "the music of words," as distinct from "songs without words" or "music alone." How to put this more generally? If we define song with Saint Thomas Aquinas as "the leap of mind in the eternal breaking out into sound" (*exultatio mentis de aeternis habita prorumpens in vocem*), the definition seems to be primarily about sacred song, and that indeed is what Saint Thomas has in mind, as he says this in his preface to the Psalms. It can also be true of secular song, though, if we think of time as "a changing image of eternity."

Going from song to dance came for me with my song cycle "The Church of the Poor Devil," and my first dancer was Lisa DeBoer; then "The Golden Key," and my dancer then was Kathy Turner. After that I had several dancers at a time, in "The Well at the World's End" and "The Green Child" and "Songlines of the Gospel." I didn't dance myself but played the piano in these performances, but I felt I was participating in the exultation of the dance. I suppose the essential thing here is going from words to music. Rhythm is the element common to words and music, and rhythm is the essence of the dance. Learning to love with all your might is learning to love with your body, with bodily movements that are rhythmical. I left the choreography to the dancers, contenting myself with writing the words and the music, and directing the song and dance from the piano.

If my road taken is the way of words, my road not taken rejoining the road taken is the way of song that becomes also the way of dance. I take it primarily, though, as the way of song, for that is a synthesis of words and music. My first steps on this way were to compose song cycles. My next step, the one I am taking now, is to compose a symphony of songs, to compose for voice and orchestra.

The Road Not Taken

"Song is the leap of mind in the eternal breaking out into sound." Those words of Saint Thomas Aquinas in his preface to the Psalms are my guiding principle in bringing together the way of words and the way of music. *Canticum est exultatio mentis,* "Song is the leap of mind" or "the exultation of mind," *de aeternis habita,* "on eternal things" or "upon the eternal," *prorumpens in vocem,* "breaking out into sound" or "into voice." That is a more literal translation of his Latin. The eternal itself does not break out into sound but the leap of mind, the exultation of mind over the eternal. Exultation or exultance is joy or jubilation and exultation or exultance over the eternal is joy or jubilation over the eternal, joy at the thought of God, the very definition, according to Spinoza, of the love of God.

A symphony of songs is a twentieth-century form, as far as I know, for instance Stravinsky's *Symphony of Psalms* for chorus and orchestra (1930) and Górecki's *Symphony of Sorrowful Songs* for soprano and orchestra (1976). (So there can be sorrowful songs. Yet they do not express simply the emotion of sorrow but "emotion recollected in tranquillity.") My own "Symphony of Songs" is for soprano and string orchestra (2003), and it consists of seven songs and is divided like Stravinsky's and Górecki's into three movements. All the songs were used before in song cycles for voice and piano, what is new is the string orchestra and the symphonic form. There is *music as a state of being,* as in tribal music and in jazz, and there is *music as symbolic form,*[20] and that is what I am seeking, to give joy at the thought of God symbolic form.

Before trying to do the "Symphony of Songs" I tried orchestrating a Dance of the Elves I had written as a piano piece when I was a teenager. Here indeed I was taking "the path taken by the soul of the dancer." I had used this piece in a song and dance cycle called "The Church of the Poor Devil." There I called it "The Dance of the Spirits" and Lisa DeBoer danced it like a spirit in 1992. Now I wanted to arrange it for orchestra and I returned to the original name, thinking also of Tolkien, The Dance of the Elves. It came out very well, as far as I can tell, though I have only heard it played back by my computer, sounding more like an accordion than an orchestra.

Arranging my "Symphony of Songs" for string orchestra, I thought of Arnold Schoenberg's *Transfigured Night* (*Verklärte Nacht*) for string orchestra in its later revision (1943). But I can see how complex his composition is and how simple mine is. I am counting on the songs of the soprano to be "the leap of mind in the eternal breaking out into sound" while the string orchestra is mostly accompaniment. It is only the opening section, purely orchestral, that sounds like a traditional symphony.

"There is a dream dreaming us." That is the theme of the first of my seven songs. It is a Bushman saying that Laurens van der Post records in *The Heart of the Hunter.* He was pressing the Bushmen in Africa to talk about the beginning of the world, until one night his favorite hunter replied, "But you see, it is very difficult, for always there is a dream dreaming us."[21] Laurens van der Post compares this saying to that of Saint John, "In the beginning was the Word." "Believing as I do that the dream is not a waste product of the mind expelled through some sewage system of the spirit but a manifestation of first and abiding meaning," van der Post explains, "I thought I should enlarge Saint John's theme to include the idea that in the beginning there was a dream. This dream was with God and indeed was God. Somehow the dream demanded that it should be lived. As Saint John might have put it, the dream was made flesh."[22]

My own song on this sings of the four states of mind that are mentioned in the Upanishads: waking, dreaming, dreamless sleep, and oneness.[23] And I sing of going back to our original oneness with things when we could understand the language of the sparrows. I was thinking of David Guss's anthology of story and song, *The Language of the Birds*,[24] and of my own experience as a child, thinking of God whenever I saw a sparrow. I imagine us going back from waking to dreaming to dreamless sleep to oneness and coming thus to know the larger story we are in. I was thinking too, like van der Post, of the Gospel of Saint John and how it starts, "In the beginning was the Word," and those became the words of my second song.

"My name, and yours," Ursula LeGuin says in one of her stories, "and the true name of the sun, or a spring of water, or an unborn child, all are syllables of the great word that is very slowly spoken by the shining of the stars."[25] That is the Word that was in the beginning, I believe, and though it sounds like a multisyllabic word here, I think all those syllables are compressed into one simple sentence like "I am" in the Gospel of Saint John and then again broken down in Christ's teaching into "the words of eternal life," as when many were leaving him and Jesus said to the twelve "Do you also wish to go away?" and Peter said "Lord, to whom shall we go? You have the words of eternal life."[26]

My second song then is simply the prologue of Saint John set to music, "In the beginning was the Word, and the Word was with God, and the Word was God." But then in the next lines there is a change. Instead of "He" I say "This," meaning the Word, "This was in the beginning with God; all came to be through this, and without this nothing came that ever came to be."[27] I don't want to say "He" until "the Word became flesh and dwelt among us" as Jesus Christ. But I end with the ending of the prologue, "In this was life, and the life was the light of humankind, and the light shines in the darkness, and the darkness has not overshadowed it." I think the incarnation is there in "the light shines in the darkness," and the resurrection is there in "the darkness has not overshadowed it." I borrowed that last phrase from Peter Levi's translation.[28] I was surprised that none of the great composers like Bach or Mozart have set the prologue of Saint John to music, only Josquin Desprez.[29]

Those two songs and the orchestral introduction are the first movement of my "Symphony of Songs." The second movement consists of three more songs and I call them "Romantic Variations on a Theme of Palestrina." The theme is that of his motet and mass *Ascendo ad Patrem*.[30] The motet is a musical setting of the words of Jesus to Mary Magdalene, "I am ascending to my Father and your Father, to my God and your God."[31] It has always been a favorite melody for me, just improvising on the piano, for it soars like an ascension. It is indeed a "leap of mind in the eternal breaking out into sound."

My third song then, "In the Lost Hills," is a musical variation on this theme, but the words are addressed to the figure of Holy Wisdom, as this song was originally part of my first song cycle, dedicated to Holy Wisdom whom I call Ayasofya, using the Turkish derivative of the Greek Hagia Sophia.[32] I sing of finding her in a human heart, in the human heart of a person I loved and lost, and hoping to meet her again "as child and child" and then again "face to face" and then again "as friend and friend," like the three meetings with her Vladimir Solovyov describes in his poem "Three Meetings."[33] I call this a "romantic" variation on the theme because I originally met Holy Wisdom not in herself but in the human heart of a person I loved and lost. I got the name "Lost Hills" from a town I went through once, and used it because I had lost the person I loved.

All the same, the song is full of hope of meeting Holy Wisdom, and my fourth song is a dance, "Rainbow Dance" I call it, from my song cycle "The Golden Key,"[34] and is the nearest of the three variations to the original melody of Palestrina, though it too is a variation, and the words are a *haiku* of seventeen syllables,

> I can see
> the rainbow in my heart
> when all my eyes see
> is the dark.

I was thinking of the saying, "Faith is seeing light with your heart when all your eyes see is darkness."[35] So here I've gone from romance to faith, though there is still an echo of romance in the phrase "when all my eyes see is the dark."

My fifth song then, "Heart's Desire," the third of these romantic variations on a theme of Palestrina, is from my song cycle "The Well at the World's End."[36] It contains my break with romance where I sing "An earthly friend I know

now cannot be my Beatrice, my Laura, only Ayasofya can."
I realize here the transcendence of longing, how the heart's
longing always goes beyond any finite object, even "an
earthly friend," how it can only be fulfilled by a transcendent object, how "our heart is restless until it rests in thee,"
as Saint Augustine prays at the beginning of his *Confessions*. So I realize at this point how the transcendence of
our longing can ruin a human relationship if we turn it on
another human being, and how we can save the human re-
lationships of our lives only by turning to God, *being with*
the other human person rather than *facing* the other with
our heart's desire.

After this comes the third movement of my "Symphony
of Songs," consisting of two songs from my first song cycle
dedicated to Ayasofya, the figure of Holy Wisdom. Both
songs have the same melody, one that I thought of many
years ago and originally intended as the Kyrie Eleison of a
mass.[37] The first of these two songs, "Shadow of God," the
sixth song of this Symphony, has the same melody as that
original Kyrie and has a second theme that was to be
the Christe Eleison. Here, though, the words are parallel to
those of the Ave Maria:

All hail, wisdom	Hail Mary,
of silence and the dark,	full of grace,
you are with God	the Lord is with you.
and your bliss is with us	Blessed are you among women,
and we are blessed.	and blessed is the fruit of your
	womb, Jesus.
All holy wisdom,	Holy Mary,
shadow of God,	Mother of God,
be with me,	pray for us sinners,
always at work in me.	now and at the hour of our death.

There is something of sonata form in this third movement as well as in the first movement of my "Symphony of Songs," as in a traditional symphony. There are in both of these movements a principal theme and a secondary theme, then a development of one of the themes, and then a recapitulation. The difference, of course, is in the themes being sung. The two themes in this last movement are both sung in "Shadow of God," and then the development and recapitulation take place in the last song "Ayasofya." As a song, however, this last is purely melismatic like an "Alleluia" in Gregorian Chant, nothing but the word itself "Ayasofya" with all its open vowels. My sopranos singing my song cycles have loved it and used it as warmup, as it covers the whole soprano range from middle C to high A.

"Ayasofya" then, my seventh and last song, takes the principal theme of "Shadow of God" and sends it through a series of harmonic changes like those of Bach's Prelude in C.[38] I count that as development and recapitulation and thus as completing the sonata form of this last movement. I suppose the most unusual thing about this is even to have a hymn to Holy Wisdom. There is an antiphon in the Liturgy of the Hours, "Wisdom of God, be with me, always at work in me," along with a canticle from the Book of Wisdom.[39] And there are biblical passages on the figure of Wisdom in the Book of Proverbs, recognized as canonical by all, and there is especially the one passage in the Book of Wisdom (or the Wisdom of Solomon), counted as apocryphal by some, where her twenty-one attributes are named, "For in her there is a spirit that is intelligent, holy, unique, manifold, subtle, mobile, clear, unpolluted, distinct, invulnerable, loving the good, keen, irresistible, beneficent, humane, steadfast, sure, free from anxiety, all-powerful, overseeing all, and penetrating through all spirits that are intelligent and pure and most subtle."[40]

Another thing that is unusual is to actually name the figure of Holy Wisdom with a proper name, as I am doing here, though the proper name is derived from the common name. "Eternal friend, I shall not name you,"[41] Solovyov says at the beginning and again at the end of his poem about his three meetings with her. I am making bold here to name her "Ayasofya," using the Turkish name for the place in Istanbul that was a church for a thousand years with the Greek name "Hagia Sophia" or "Holy Wisdom" and then a mosque for five hundred years with this Turkish name derived from the Greek, "Ayasofya." I have turned the place name into a personal name. But somehow naming her enhances the possibility of a relationship with her, and that is what I desire and am seeking here.

There is in this relationship with the figure of Holy Wisdom an answer to the romantic problem of love and loss, "An earthly friend I know now cannot be my Beatrice, my Laura, only Ayasofya can." It is then a way in which the Road Not Taken of romantic love rejoins the Road Taken of learning to love "with all your heart, and with all your soul, and with all your might." The wholeness of the love of God seems to encompass the lost romantic love. Dante's Beatrice, though she was in life "an earthly friend," becomes after death for him an embodiment of Lady Wisdom, and in the *Divine Comedy* when she smiles a last time and then looks toward God, he follows her gaze and never looks back.[42] When Petrarca first saw Laura, "Was this when the Renaissance began?" James Hillman asks, "Or had it already begun" when Dante first saw Beatrice?[43]

"These couples, Petrarca and Laura, Dante and Beatrice, had no personal satisfaction, no human relationship,"
Hillman says. "Yet what emerged from these happenings in
the heart was the transformation of all Western culture."[44]
If we take into account the transcendence of longing, we
can see why they "had no personal satisfaction, no human
relationship." At the same time we can see why "from
these happenings in the heart" there came "the transformation of all Western culture" in the Renaissance. "We can
know more than we can tell,"[45] Michael Polanyi says, and
we do so by "dwelling in the particulars" of what we know.
The method of the Renaissance, however, the method of
Leonardo da Vinci for instance, was to focus on those particulars. If we focus on the particulars in this way, then
the transcendent becomes "the tacit dimension" of our
knowing.

"Obstinate Rigor" (*ostinato rigore*),[46] that was Leonardo's motto, and I see it carried out in his dwelling on the
particulars in painting and sculpture and architecture
and invention and in everything he did. This method could
also be used in drama, like Shakespeare speaking or having
one of his characters speaking of "the particulars of my
life."[47] Indeed the transcendent is "the tacit dimension" of
Shakespeare's plays. "We can know more than we can tell"
seems true of Shakespeare's plays and Leonardo's paint-
ings, for instance of Leonardo's Mona Lisa. After finish-
ing my studies in Rome (1957) I came to Paris and stayed
at a house where I was the only English-speaking guest,
and it became my task to take English-speaking visitors
there on a tour of Paris. I always ended the tour at the
Louvre in front of the Mona Lisa, and each time I seemed
to meet someone or other there who wanted to discuss the

existence of God—as if the enigmatic smile of the Mona Lisa held some secret.

If we focus on the secret of our lives, on our relation to the things of our life, rather than on the things themselves, then "the tacit dimension" becomes the particulars of our life. The articulate or spoken dimension is the "transcendental" as Kant calls it to distinguish it from God the "transcendent." That is the focus of my "Symphony of Songs," the transcendence of our longing and the transcendent itself in the shape of the Word and Ayasofya. What this leads us to is a conception or a vision of a deeper life of knowledge and love that transcends the particulars of our life, that leads us beyond the horizon of the things of life entering our lives and passing from our lives.

A DEEPER LIFE

Most people don't have a rich inner life.
—remark of Henri Nouwen
to the author

"I believe there is a life in the Eucharist that can live on through death," Sister Margaret Farley once said to me. She was echoing "the words of eternal life" in John 6, but her remark led me to see that the question of eternal life is not simply "Is there a life after death?" but rather "Is there a life in us now that can live on through death?" If there is such a life, I began to see, it has to be the inner life of knowledge and love.

"Most people don't have a rich inner life," Henri Nouwen once said to me, speaking of Dag Hammarskjöld and the rich inner life that appears in *Markings*. The loneliness that appears there also ("loneliness" is the most frequent word besides "and," "the," and "but") is apparently compatible with a rich inner life, though you might have expected the inner richness to take away the loneliness. Henri himself was similar, it seemed to me, he had a rich inner life but was very lonely. A rich inner life, as I understand it, is a life of hope and peace and friends and intelligence. Henri had that, as did Hammarskjöld, but in spite of the hope and the peace, in spite even of the many friends he had, he was very lonely. Was it the intelligence that made him so? It is one thing to be alone, and it is another to know that you are alone. Loneliness is being alone, and knowing you are alone, and longing to be unalone.

There is a connection between loneliness and love, I have learned, the longing in the loneliness can become love, I mean, as in the African love song "I walk alone."[1] It can become not only romantic love but even the love of God. That is why I want to call the longing *the heart's desire.* There is an ascent of the heart to God that goes along with the ascent of the mind to God. The mind's ascent is from *phenomena* to *noumena,* as for instance in Heidegger's in-tellectual journey "through phenomenology to thought,"[2] and it can become an ascent of the mind to God when "thinking is thanking" (*Denken ist Danken*).[3] The heart's ascent, as I understand it, is from longing to love, where love is essentially joy at the thought of the loved one. So when the mind comes to thinking and thanking, the heart may come to joy. I know Heidegger was not a religious thinker, but I can see how his intellectual road can lead the mind and heart to God.

If we think of prayer as the raising of the mind and the heart to God, we can think of the ascent of the mind and heart to God as prayer or as learning to pray, like Saint Au-gustine's going from his *Soliloquies,* where he converses with himself and can only manage a brief prayer "May I know me, may I know thee" (*noverim me, noverim te*),[4] to his *Confessions,* ten years later, where he converses with God in sustained prayer. Let us take now our own road of ascent.

The Mind's Ascent to God

There are as many ways to God as there are spiritual traditions. Saint Bonaventure's *The Mind's Journey to God*[5] is in the tradition of Saint Francis of Assisi and his Canticle of the Sun. Saint Robert Bellarmine's *Ascent of the Mind to God*[6] is in the tradition of Saint Ignatius of Loyola and his *Spiritual Exercises*. I will take the approach of Saint Augustine, going from the standpoint before self, as in his *Soliloquies,* to the standpoint before God, as in his *Confessions,* but I will begin with the standpoint before others, as in Newman's *Apologia*. By taking *the sense of I* as my approach, I can connect not only with all that comes out of *I think therefore I am* but also with the *I am* sayings of the Scriptures and even with Self and No Self in Hinduism and Buddhism.

Going "through phenomenology to thought," or as Heidegger amends the phrase, "through phenomenology to the thinking of Being"[7] can lead to Being rather than to God. It would lead to God only if we assume with Meister Eckhart "Being is God" (*Esse est Deus*).[8] What Heidegger means by "Being," I gather, is what Wittgenstein means by "the mystical," saying "Not *how* the world is, is the mystical, but *that* it is."[9] That is not God unless we assume God gives his own existence to the world, something that Saint Thomas Aquinas denies when he says *Deus non est esse formale omnium,* "God is not the formal existence of all."[10] Instead God gives the world its own existence. Still, the wonder of existence, *that* it is, implies God. I think of my experience in childhood, looking up into the starry sky on a summer night, feeling the wonder of existence, the wonder of the world's existence, the wonder also of my own existence, *that* it is, *that* I am. But here this way to God joins the way I have been talking about, through *the sense of I am.*

"The contemplation of the world *sub specie aeterni* is its contemplation as a limited whole," Wittgenstein goes on to say, and "The feeling of the world as a limited whole is the mystical feeling."[11] Being, as Heidegger understands it, commenting on Parmenides,[12] is indeed a limited whole, and thus is not God who is infinite. All the same, the limited whole implies God, as the limited implies the unlimited. Moreover, the contemplation of the world *sub specie aeterni* and the feeling of the world as a limited whole, the contemplation and the feeling, the mystical feeling, belong to *the sense of I.*

"There is indeed the inexpressible," Wittgenstein adds. "This *shows* itself; it is the mystical."[13] Here he is making his distinction between saying and showing. Heidegger too speaks in this way of Being, saying that it shows itself and withdraws. "That which shows itself and at the same time withdraws is the essential trait of what we call the mystery."[14] *The sense of I* appears here when we ask, to whom does it show itself? from whom does it withdraw? And God shows himself and at the same time withdraws, and the Hebrew term for the withdrawal is *zimzum.* I want to say now that God shows himself and withdraws in the standpoint before others, in the standpoint before self, and in the standpoint before God.

"We can know more than we can tell," Polanyi's maxim that I keep quoting, is a key to the standpoint before others. There is a showing in what we can tell, and there is a hiding or withdrawing in what we can know and cannot tell. Newman's *Apologia,* as "a history of his religious opinions,"[15] its subtitle, can even be seen as God showing himself, insofar as it is a truthful narration, but also as a

withdrawing of God or a hiding of God insofar as Newman's privacy remains inviolate. Newman can know more
than he can tell, and I too, if I were to write a history of my
religious opinions, can know more than I can tell, and so
God in this telling would be showing himself and at the
same time withdrawing in Newman's knowing more and
my own knowing more. What we can tell is the story; what
we can know, more than we can tell, I believe, is the relationship, our relationship with God.

"Commit thy way to the Lord and trust in Him, and He
will do it. And He will bring forth thy justice as the light,
and thy judgement as the noon day."[16] Those verses from
the psalm are the epigraph of Newman's *Apologia*. Another
translation is "Commit your way to the Lord and put your
trust in Him, and He will bring it to pass. He will make
your righteousness as clear as the light, and your just deal-
ing as the noonday."[17] What this is about is God backing
the person before others, if you commit your way to God
and trust in God, He will back you before others. If I
commit my way to God and trust in God, God will be with
me as I stand before others. Newman was under attack
from Charles Kingsley, and his *Apologia* is an answer to the
charge of insincerity, a difficult thing to answer if *we can
know more than we can tell,* for sincerity can be the require-
ment that we *tell all.*

As it is, we can tell the story: Newman can recount
"a history of his religious opinions," and I can tell the story
of my learning to love God, first with all my mind, coming
to a peaceful vision of all coming from God and all returning to God, then with all my heart, realizing I will die someday and finding in "the words of eternal life" an answer to
death, then with all my soul, learning detachment in love
by going through love and loss, and then with all my might

like David who "danced before the Lord with all his might" as the way of words and the way of music come together in my life. The story in this way is "the truth, the whole truth, and nothing but the truth." Still, there is what is told and what is untold in the story.

What is untold in the story, what we can know that is more than we can tell, according to Polanyi, comes of "dwelling in the particulars"[18] of what we know. The particulars of a life are many, more than we could ever tell, but our dwelling in them is our relation to them and that can be one. By relating to myself and willing to be myself, Kierkegaard says, I am grounded transparently in God ("By relating itself to its own self and by willing to be itself the self is grounded transparently in the Power which posited it").[19] My dwelling in the particulars of my life is my relating to myself. This belongs to my standpoint before myself rather than my standpoint before others and so is a "tacit dimension," as Polanyi calls it, in my standpoint before others. What is untold in my story thus is what belongs to my standpoint before myself and my standpoint before God, and is essentially my relation to myself and my relation to God.

When I pass from the standpoint before others to the standpoint before myself, I am freed of the hopes and fears that belong to the standpoint before others, the hopes of acceptance, the fears of rejection by others. "Poetry is the spontaneous overflow of powerful feelings," Wordsworth says: "it takes its origin from emotion recollected in tranquillity."[20] That recollection in tranquillity takes place, I believe, in the standpoint before self. There is recollection also in the standpoint before others but its tranquillity is disturbed by hopes and fears about one's standing with others. It is when I pass to the standpoint before myself that I can recollect emotion in tranquillity, for instance when I am writing in a diary.

There can be prayer too in the standpoint before self, like Saint Augustine's prayer in his *Soliloquies*, "May I know me! May I know thee!" but not sustained prayer as in his *Confessions*. Instead it is brief prayer, after the fashion of *The Cloud of Unknowing*, where it is said "Short prayer penetrates heaven."[21] There is brief prayer and then a return to the ongoing dialogue with oneself. What is this dialogue about? It is a conversation with oneself about all one's concerns, one's hopes and fears, even though the hopes and fears are recollected in tranquillity. It is ultimately about the heart's desire for eternal life, like Saint Augustine's conversation with himself in his *Soliloquies* about the immortality of the soul. My own question in conversation with myself was the one I formulated in my first book, "If I must die someday, what can I do to satisfy my desire to live?"—a preliminary formulation of the heart's desire—and the answer I found was in "the words of eternal life."

Eternal life and "the words of eternal life" set me on the way to realizing "God is my desire," as Tolstoy wrote in his diary, to realizing the transcendence of longing, how the heart's longing always goes beyond any finite object. But what does it mean to say "God is my desire"? "I must have wanted to say: 'God is my desire to know Him . . . No, not that . . .'" as Tolstoy started to reply to Max Gorky. What then? The desire to know God is characteristic of the standpoint before self. "May I know me! May I know thee!" is the prayer of the *Soliloquies*. The desire to know God goes with the desire to know myself. The mystery of God goes with the mystery of myself to me, that I can't leap over my own shadow. So then I pray to know myself, to know

God. "How can the knower be known?"[22] is the question
of the *Upanishads.*

An answer could be Kierkegaard's formula, by relating
to myself and willing to be myself I am grounded transparently in God (Again, "By relating itself to its own self and
by willing to be itself the self is grounded transparently in
the Power which posited it"). The mystery, though, is still
there, relating to myself and willing to be myself means
recognizing and accepting the mystery of myself, that I
can't leap over my own shadow, and being grounded transparently in God means recognizing and accepting the mystery of God. The transparency is in this, that the mystery
"shows itself" (Wittgenstein) or it "shows itself and at the
same time withdraws" (Heidegger). The relating and the
willing and the grounding then is expressed in the prayer
"May I know me! May I know thee!"

Prayer is the answer to this prayer, the standpoint of
the person before God, that of Saint Augustine in his *Confessions,* for in that standpoint I come to know myself and
I come to know God. "Thinking is thanking" in this standpoint, that is I recollect my life in the presence of God with
thanksgiving, like Dag Hammarskjöld saying "For all that
has been—Thanks! To all that shall be—Yes!" There is a
kind of formula for this in Philippians: "Rejoice in the Lord
alway: and again I say, Rejoice. Let your moderation be
known unto all men. The Lord is at hand. Be careful for
nothing; but in every thing by prayer and supplication with
thanksgiving let your requests be made known unto God.
And the peace of God, which passeth all understanding,
shall keep your hearts and minds through Christ Jesus."[23]
The formula is one of rejoicing in the Lord, the essence of
the love of God as joy at the thought of God, bringing all

your cares to God with thanksgiving, and coming thereby to a peace that passes all understanding.

"May I know me!" is answered here by recollection in the presence of God. Recollection in the presence of God is more than recollection in the presence of self or recollection in the presence of others. "Emotion recollected in tranquillity" goes over into "his will is our peace." It is indeed "the peace of God, which passeth all understanding," all understanding, that is, from the standpoint before others and the standpoint before self. I think again of Newman's epigraph from the psalm, trusting in God to justify him before others, but then I think of Milton's aim "to justify the ways of God,"[24] and it seems to me that the justification of the ways of God is in the peace that passes all understanding. The standpoint before God contains and surpasses, it seems, the standpoint before others and the standpoint before self. Saint Augustine is talking to us and to himself as well as to God in his *Confessions,* but he is seeking "the peace of God, which passeth all understanding."

"May I know thee!" is answered in the very prayer itself by the *I and thou* of prayer. Saint Augustine's answer in his *Confessions* is from the Psalms where God is addressed as "thou." It is true, certain psalms are more important to him, especially Psalm 4 ("Lift up the light of thy countenance upon us, O Lord") and Psalm 42 ("As a hart longs for flowing streams, so longs my soul for thee, O God") and Psalm 139 ("O Lord, thou hast searched me and known me!").[25] In his background, as he tells us, there are the Manichees and the (Neo)Platonists. The Manichees had psalms of their own, but the (Neo)Platonists referred to God in the third person as the One. Saint Augustine rejects the Manichee idea of God having extension in space and accepts the (Neo)Platonist idea of God as spiritual substance, as being in accord with the Gospel, "God is spirit" (John 4:24).

I find a similar problem as I read Spinoza, who understands God as substance, the one and only substance, with two attributes, thought and extension. What I like in Spinoza is his idea of the love of God as joy at the thought of God. But I have to disagree with his idea of extension as one of the two attributes of God. Instead I want to go with the Gospel of John and say "God is spirit." So only thought and not extension would be an attribute of God. What of Spinoza's basic idea of God as substance? I want to agree here with Saint Augustine that God transcends the categories, including that of substance, though we can speak of the substance of God as spirit. In all this I want to be guided as Saint Augustine was by Holy Scripture and to affirm basically an I *and thou* relation with God rather than an I *and it*.

I come thus in my mind's ascent to God to a personal God, I *and thou,* rather than an impersonal God, I *and it.* I come to God thus in terms of our relationship with God. "We can know more than we can tell," but that "more" is our relation with God not God apart from our relationship. Thus the attributes I come to are immanence and transcendence, immanence or presence to us and transcendence corresponding to the transcendence of our heart's longing. Immanence goes with the idea that the mystical "shows itself," as Wittgenstein says, and transcendence with the idea that the mystery "shows itself and at the same time withdraws," as Heidegger says. Prayer, that I relate to God as *thou* rather than *it*, puts immanence and transcen-

dence together, the showing and the withdrawing as a relating, God relating to us and us relating to God.

If our knowing of God is in prayer, then there is an
unknowing of God apart from prayer, as in *The Cloud of
Unknowing*, though it is "the cloud of unknowing in the
which a soul is oned with God,"[26] that is, I am oned with
God by recognizing and accepting my unknowing. So there
is prayer and there is silence, but if prayers are like songs,
silence is like songs without words. I am reminded, of
course, of Wittgenstein's conclusion, "Whereof one cannot speak, thereof one must be silent."[27] Silence speaks,
though, as I am saying, like songs without words. "We all
have within us a center of stillness surrounded by silence,"
the opening sentence of Dag Hammarskjöld's brochure for
the Meditation Room at the UN, suggests that there is a
significant silence in all of us, and that silence sings of God
in a song without words. It is a silence of unknowing in
which a soul is oned with God. If song, as Saint Thomas
says, is "the leap of mind in the eternal breaking out into
sound," song without words too is a leap of mind consciously unknowing in the eternal breaking out into sound.

"Everything depends on whether God has spoken
to man or if the Absolute remains silence beyond all
words," Hans Urs von Balthasar has said.[28] That the mystical "shows itself," that the mystery "shows itself and at the
same time withdraws" means "God has spoken" though
"the Absolute remains silence beyond all words." I mean
the showing and the withdrawal can be interpreted as
speech, though Wittgenstein contrasts saying and showing,
our saying and *its* showing, the mystical's showing, that
is. Standing in an *I and thou* relation with God, I take the
showing and the withdrawing as communication. "God

speaks everyday, but we don't listen," Gandhi says.[29] God speaks, I believe he means, when the heart speaks. Or God speaks when words, especially the words of Holy Scripture, speak to the heart.

"Where the story-teller is loyal, eternally and unswervingly loyal to the story, there in the end, silence will speak," as Isak Dinesen says. "Where the story has been betrayed, silence is but emptiness."[30] Thus Saint Augustine recollecting his life before God is loyal to the story, and in his writings after his *Confessions* the silence speaks. I have always wondered why he does not continue to write in the mode of prayer in his later works, but I think I see now that the silence is speaking in them and through them. His works before his *Confessions* are mostly unfinished, as if he had a writer's block of some kind, but after his *Confessions* there is no block. And I suppose you could say the silence is speaking or the heart is speaking.

The Silence of the Heart Speaks

"Who can understand the omnipotent Trinity?" Saint Augustine asks at the end of his *Confessions*. "People debate and quarrel," he says, "and without peace no one sees that vision."[31] After his *Confessions* Saint Augustine goes on to write *On the Trinity*, but as he says here "without peace no one sees that vision." I take it that the heart speaking is like poetry, as Wordsworth says, "Poetry is the spontaneous overflow of powerful feelings: it takes its origin from emotion recollected in tranquillity." Recollection in tranquillity is essential here, it seems, if "without peace no one sees that vision." It is not emotion that is recollected, however, but being, knowing, and willing, being corresponding to the Father, knowing to the Son, and willing to the Holy Spirit.

"For I am and I know and I will," Saint Augustine explains. These three are distinct and yet one. "Knowing and willing I am. I know that I am and I will. I will to be and to know."[32] That is his image of the Trinity in the human mind, the mental trinity he describes in his *Confessions.* Later in his book *On the Trinity* he describes several more mental trinities: the lover and the beloved and the love, the mind itself and its love and its knowledge, and finally memory and understanding and will, all of them, I believe, derivatives of his original trio, being and knowing and willing.

Does the heart speak on the Trinity? Although it is not emotion that is being recollected here in tranquillity, still being, knowing, and willing are not without emotion. They are what Pascal calls "reasons of the heart." "Emotion is the chief source of all becoming-conscious," Jung says. "There can be no transforming of darkness into light and of apathy into movement without emotion."[33] Here we have Saint Augustine's mental trinity, being and knowing and willing, or in its final form in *On the Trinity*, memory and understanding and will. "Emotion is the chief source of all becoming-conscious," and that is being or memory. "There can be no transforming of darkness into light," and that is knowing or understanding, "and of apathy into movement," and that is willing or will, "without emotion."

We seem to be rather far from the Trinity, Father and Son and Holy Spirit, talking about this mental trinity. If we think of it as *presence,* though, rather than simply analogy, then we are talking about the Trinity, the indwelling of the Father and the Son and the Holy Spirit. But is memory the presence of the Father, understanding the presence of the Son, and will the presence of the Holy Spirit? It is, or it can be, I want to say, when as in Newman's motto "heart speaks to heart."

There is a pattern here somewhat like the one we found in the mind's ascent to God: the person before others, the person before self, and the person before God. "One human heart goes out to another undeterred by what lies between," Grimm's saying, and "From the heart may it go to the heart," Beethoven's for his *Kyrie eleison,* and "heart to heart" the common phrase in many languages, for instance the Indonesian (?) *hati ke hati,* all describe one human heart speaking to another human heart.[34] This may already be God speaking, if God speaks when the heart speaks. Gandhi's saying, though, "God speaks every day, but we don't listen," brings out the need for listening, as in Malebranche's saying "Attention is the natural prayer of the soul." The image and the presence of the Trinity appears here in the heart speaking, or God speaking his eternal Word, and us under the influence of his Holy Spirit, listening with attention, the natural prayer of the soul.

There are two processes here, or two processions (to use the term used in the doctrine of the Trinity), the speaking and the listening. God spoke one Word and then he kept silence, Saint John of the Cross says ("For in giving us, as He did, His Son, which is His Word—and He has no other—He spoke to us all together, once and for all, in this single Word, and He has no occasion to speak further").[35] But that Word is spoken, if I am on the right track here, every time the heart speaks, every time heart speaks to heart. When I say "the heart speaks" or when Newman says "heart speaks to heart," we have in mind the heart's desire, as when Tolstoy says "God is my desire" or Saint Augustine says "our heart is restless until it rest in thee." Understanding it this way, we can say every time the heart speaks, every time heart speaks to heart, God speaks and the eternal Word is spoken. There we have the answer to von Balthasar's question, "Everything depends on whether God has spoken to man or if the Absolute remains silence beyond words." It is true then, God spoke one Word and then kept silence, but that one Word is spoken again and again when the heart speaks or heart speaks to heart, and apart from that one Word "the Absolute remains silence beyond words."

Listening, the other process or procession, can mean discerning the true names of things. I think again of Ursula LeGuin's saying, "My name and yours, and the true name of the sun, or a spring of water, or an unborn child, all are syllables of the great word that is very slowly spoken by the shining of the stars." Listening with attention, the natural prayer of the soul, can also mean listening to the silence as to a song without words. "The wind bloweth where it listeth, and thou hearest the sound thereof," Jesus says of the Holy Spirit, "but canst not tell whence it cometh, and whither it goeth."[36] (I use KJ instead of RSV here because it says "tell" rather than "know.") Here again "we can know more than we can tell." Listening to the divine wind of the Spirit, we cannot tell where it comes from or where it is going, but we can know it comes from the unknown and it is going into the unknown. We can know it is coming from God, that is, and going to God. Here again we encounter "the cloud of unknowing in the which a soul is oned with God." We are oned with God in recognizing the unknown whence and whither of the Spirit.

"To Hear Thoroughly," the memoir of Father Dunstan Morrissey, tells of this process of listening in the life of a hermit, and describes a remarkable dream he had when he was in India. He saw two semicircular arches in a railway station in Bombay like theatre marquees. One said Saguna Brahman or God with attributes; the other said Nirguna Brahman or God without attributes.[37] He didn't know which way to go. Finally he decided the dream was about waiting. He was to wait on God and let God reveal God. The mystical, as Wittgenstein says, "shows itself"; the mystery, as Heidegger says, "shows itself and at the same time withdraws." To listen or "to hear thoroughly" is to let the mystical show, to let the mystery show and withdraw.

All through the course of time this process goes on, the mystical showing itself, the mystery showing and withdrawing. This in effect is the process Saint Augustine is describing in *The City of God*. "Let me confess to you what I find in your books," he prays in his *Confessions*. "'Let me hear the voice of praise' and drink you, and let me consider 'wonderful things out of your law'—from the beginning in which you made heaven and earth until the perpetual reign with you in your heavenly city."[38] That is an outline of what he says afterwards in *The City of God*, but here I am staying with what he says of it in prayer in his *Confessions*, like what he says there also of the Trinity, still wondering why he doesn't continue in those later books to speak in the mode of prayer. I want to compare and contrast the story he tells in *The City of God* with a recent scientific wall chart I've seen called "The History and Fate of the Universe."[39]

I suppose the basic difference is in the words of Wittgenstein, "Not *how* the world is, is the mystical, but *that* it is." The wall chart "The History and Fate of the Universe" is about *how* the world is; *The City of God* is about the mystical, *that* it is. I think what Saint Augustine is doing in *The City of God*, at least in the second half (Books XI to XXII), is reading the Bible through, end to end, and letting it speak to his heart. It is what the monks later called *lectio divina,* divine reading. In his *Confessions* he is speaking to God; in *The City of God* he is letting God speak to him, or letting God speak to his heart. I see I have the answer here to why he is not writing there in the mode of prayer. In fact, it *is* in the mode of prayer, if prayer is conversation with God, conversation in which we not only speak to God but God speaks also to us.

Why a city? Rome was sacked in 410, and he began writing *The City of God* three years later in 413 and finished it in 427, just three years before he died, with the Vandals at the gate of his little town of Hippo. He was inspired to answer the pagan critics (books 1 to 10) who blamed the fall of Rome on Christianity much as Edward Gibbon, centuries later, felt inspired to blame it on Christianity. "It was at Rome, on the 15th of October, 1769, as I sat musing amidst the ruins of the Capitol, while the barefoot friars were singing vespers in the Temple of Jupiter," Gibbon writes in his autobiography, "that the idea of writing the decline and fall of the city first started to my mind."[40]

Either way it was a tale of two cities, and Saint Augustine in his time and Gibbon in his time and we in our time can say like Charles Dickens in *A Tale of Two Cities,*

It was the best of times, it was the worst of times, it was the age of wisdom, it was the age of foolishness, it was the epoch of belief, it was the epoch of incredulity, it was the season of Light, it was the season of Darkness, it was the spring of hope, it was the winter of despair, we had everything before us, we had nothing before us, we were all going direct to Heaven, we were all going direct the other way.[41]

That's the way it looks in the standpoint before ourselves. If we pass over into the standpoint before God, however, like Saint Augustine, then "heart speaks to heart" and we see a vision like he did, "from the beginning in which you made heaven and earth until the perpetual reign with you in your heavenly city."

Looking at the wall chart "The History and Fate of the Universe," and reflecting on Wittgenstein's three sentences on the mystical, I have three questions, one on each sentence. "Not *how* the world is, is the mystical, but *that* it is," his first sentence, suggests the question of the relation between *how* and *that*. If the *how* is a past, "the History," and a future, "the Fate," the *that* is a present. Or better, it is a presence. There is the presence of the universe. There is the presence of God in the universe. I think of the desperate prayer in *The Silver King,* "O God! Put back Thy universe and give me yesterday."[42] The creation of the universe is not a matter of *how* the world is, that there is a Big Bang from which it starts, but *that* it is. That seems to be Saint Augustine's thinking on "the beginning in which you made heaven and earth," and so too on the end, not a matter of a heat death of the universe but of the presence of God in "the perpetual reign with you in your heavenly city."

"The contemplation of the world subspecie aeterni is its contemplation as a limited whole" and "The feeling of the world as a limited whole is the mystical feeling," the second sentence on the mystical, suggests the question of the relation between time and eternity. If time is "a changing image of eternity," as Plato says, then this limited whole with its beginning and end is a changing image of something without beginning and end. E. E. Cummings in his poem "pity this busy monster, manunkind"[43] says

> listen: there's a hell
> of a good universe next door; let's go

Saint Augustine too has a very pessimistic view of the city of this world, believing like René Girard in our time that it is founded on murder (Cain killed Abel and founded the first city, and Romulus killed Remus and founded the city of Rome) and he is saying too in effect "let's go" to the City of God "a hell of a good universe next door." But is the City of God a "universe next door"? E. E. Cummings no doubt means this world not the other world. Saint Augustine, on the other hand, is thinking "here we have no continuing city, but we seek one to come" (Hebrews 13:14).

Still, there may be a bridge in the third sentence on the mystical, "There is indeed the inexpressible. This *shows* itself; it is the mystical." All through time the mystical is showing itself, and that is the story Saint Augustine is telling in *The City of God*. The story in brief is the one told in the last chapters of Hebrews, the story of faith. "Now faith is the substance of things hoped for, the evidence of things not seen," it begins, and then it goes on to actually name the City of God, saying Abraham the father of faith "looked for a city which hath foundations, whose builder and maker is God," and he and his children "were strangers and pilgrims on earth" desiring "a better country, that is a heavenly: wherefore God is not ashamed to be called their God: for he hath prepared for them a city," and it ends "For here have we no continuing city, but we seek one to come."[44] I gather from this way of telling the story that if the mystical shows itself, it shows itself to faith.

It shows itself in another way, or perhaps I should say it hides itself, in the mystical convergence of the great religions, the sort of thing Rudolf Otto describes in *Mysticism East and West*,[45] comparing Shankara and Meister Eckhart, something Saint Augustine did not envision. It hides itself, I will say, for the mystery, as Heidegger calls it, "shows itself and at the same time withdraws." I see the withdrawal in the experience of someone like Pascal saying "The eternal silence of these infinite spaces terrifies me."[46] That brings me back to the wall chart on "The History and Fate of the Universe." But perhaps "the eternal silence of these infinite spaces" is a song without words. The mystery shows itself in the story of faith in a song with words and it hides itself in the history and fate of the universe in a song without words. Moreover, the mystical unity of the religions is a song without words, not a verbal unity of creed or cult; it is a relationship to "the eternal silence of these infinite spaces"; it is the mysticism of "the cloud of unknowing in the which a soul is oned with God."

I borrow this term "song without words" from Mendelssohn, his eight books of *Songs without Words* (*Lieder ohne Worte*) and a later *Song without Words* (*Ein Lied ohne Worte*) written for a princess whose sister was an opera singer.[47] These are piano pieces in song form. I want to use the term as a metaphor for a significant silence. The story of faith, as told in the Bible and in Saint Augustine's *City of God,* is a song with words, but "the eternal silence of these infinite spaces," according to this metaphor, is a song without words about the history and fate of the universe. I even have my own version of this song without words in the form of a universe in which matter is a dimension along with space and time.[48]

Here too "we can know more than we can tell." We can tell the story of faith, a song with words, but we can know "the poetry of the universe"[49] as Robert Osserman calls it, a song without words, as I am calling it, where the silence speaks, even "the eternal silence of these infinite spaces." Taking time and matter as dimensions along with the three dimensions of space, we come to what is essentially a space theory of time and matter. So it is indeed "the eternal silence of these infinite spaces" that is being broken, or that is speaking in "the poetry of the universe," or that is singing in our song without words. Thus the deeper life here is the life of the mind, the contemplative mind that is, and the life of the heart, as heart speaks to heart, and the life of the soul, as the soul is oned with God in the unknowing that is knowing more than we can tell.

I hope this is not an unduly gnostic turn to interpret the unknowing in *The Cloud of Unknowing* as knowing more than we can tell. It is "the cloud of unknowing in the which a soul is oned with God." I take it that we can tell the story, the story of faith, but we can know the relationship, the *I and thou* with God, and "a soul is oned with God" in the unconditional relation of Jesus with "my Father and your Father," as he says to Mary Magdalene, "my God and your God." This is the deeper life that can live on through death. The ascent of the mind to God, from the standpoint before others to that before self to that before God, I gather, is an entering into this relationship, and it is in this relationship that heart speaks to heart.

Writing after the Renaissance, many centuries after *The City of God*, Vico saw a *ricorso* of the earthly city after the *corso* of history ending in the decline and fall of the Roman Empire that Saint Augustine saw. The *ricorso*, though, passes again through the cycle of barbarism and civilization and decadence that we see now. "For here we have no continuing city, but we seek one to come," the moral of the story we can tell, leads us on to what we can know more than we can tell, the *I and thou* with God, "I in them, and thou in me" as Christ says at the Last Supper, speaking "the words of eternal life," and this is eternal life, as he says there, to know *I in them, and thou in me,* the unconditional relation with "my Father and your Father, my God and your God." This is the inner life *now* that becomes the life after life *then*.

GOING THROUGH
DEATH TO LIFE

> In place of death there was light.
> —Tolstoy, "The Death
> of Ivan Ilych"

Meditating on the story of Jesus, his withdrawal into solitude and his return to the human circle, I thought we could enter into the essential moments of his life except for the last and most decisive of all, his going through death to life. We could not enter into that, I thought, simply because we are still alive and have yet to pass through death. Then I read "The Death of Ivan Ilych" by Tolstoy and I realized it is possible like Ivan Ilych to pass through death before we draw our last breath, that the essence of death is in letting go of everyone and everything and entering into a new relationship with everyone and everything, and that can happen before we actually die, and we can learn, as Ivan Ilych did, "In place of death there was light."[1]

Life and light and love, the three great metaphors of the Gospel of John, describe the deeper life that can live on through death, and they make sense of that sentence of Tolstoy's, "In place of death there was light." The metaphors describe eternal life, beginning already on this side and continuing on the other side of death. The life is the light, and the light is the love, and the love is "from God and of God and towards God," as the old Bedouin said to Lawrence of Arabia, but according to the Gospel of John you enter into that circle by believing, by believing in Christ who is the life and the light and the love incarnate, who is from God and of God and towards God.

"Death is not an event of life. Death is not lived through,"[2] Wittgenstein says, challenging the idea of eternal life. This is a modern thought that derives from the time of the Black Death, I believe, when death came to be seen no longer as part of life but as attacking life from the outside. Let us turn this back into a question, Is death an event of life? Is death lived through? "Is a riddle solved by the fact that I survive forever?" Wittgenstein asks. "Is this eternal life not as enigmatic as our present one?"[3] He is thinking of an afterlife. If we see eternal life not simply as afterlife but as our inner life now living on, then the question is a different one.

Instead of simply trying a Yes answer to the questions, "Is death an event of life?" and "Is death lived through?" let us consider what seems to be the essence of death, letting go of everyone and everything and a new relation with everyone and everything. If death means letting go of everyone and everything, it is an event of life, and if death means entering into a new relation with everyone and everything it is lived through.

Letting Go of Everyone and Everything

Letting go of everyone and everything in "The Death of Ivan Ilych" comes down to letting go of the justification of a life. Say my life is one of gaining and sharing insight, then the justification of my life is in gaining and sharing insight or in the insight I gain and share. Or say I seek not so much to be happy as to be worthy of happiness, as Kant says, then the justification of my life is in being worthy of happiness. That is close to Ivan Ilych's idea of the justification of his life, as Tolstoy describes him, leading a good life or a respectable life that makes him worthy of happiness. So he feels outraged by the prospect of dying. Thus he finds himself clinging to life or clinging to the justification of his life in the face of death. What happens to him then in dying is that he has to let go of the justification of his life or rather the justification is torn out of his grasp. "What hindered him from making his way through was the confession that his life had been good. This justification of his life caught him, and did not let him advance, and more than all else tormented him."[4]

At the end he wanted to say *Prosti*, "Forgive," but he said *Propusti*, "Let it pass"[5] or rather "Farewell," even "Farewell to life," as a young Russian woman translated for me. That was his letting go. "Forgive" is letting go of the past, or asking to be released from the past, and "Farewell" is letting go of life, or asking to be released from life. He asks himself then "Where is the pain?" Then he finds it and feels it and knows he is still alive. Then he asks himself "Where is death?" and he can't find it anywhere. He has already passed through death, and "In place of death there was light." For those with him his death agony lasted two more hours. Then "he drew in one more breath, stopped in the midst of it, stretched himself, and died."

It is possible to speak of letting go of everyone and everything, however, without any mention of death. Martin Heidegger has a little piece called *Gelassenheit*, "Letting Be," translated into English as *Discourse on Thinking* where "letting be" is said to be the essence of thinking.[6] The term *Gelassenheit* comes from Meister Eckhart where it means detachment of spirit—I call it being "heart-free." For Heidegger, though, with his focus on being, "letting be" comes to mean the essence of being. If "letting be" is the essence of thinking, if it is the essence of being, how can it also be the essence of dying, unless death is indeed an event of life, unless death is indeed lived through? All I can think of, trying to put all these things together are the words of Genesis, "Let there be light."[7] Those words suggest letting things be, creating them, and they could suggest letting things be in thinking, and even letting things be in dying if "In place of death there was light."

We have then three things to consider here: letting be as the essence of thinking, letting be as the essence of being, and letting be as the essence of dying. "Too many notes!"[8] as the emperor says to Mozart in *Amadeus,* there are too many meanings encoded into this one concept of letting be, but hopefully we can answer with Mozart, not too many, even all one in the unity of their symbolic form.

What is thinking? That is the question of Heidegger's *Discourse on Thinking,* and the answer is in its German title, *Gelassenheit,* "Letting Be." The Discourse is divided into two parts, a Memorial Address and a Conversation on a Country Path. The Address makes it clear that this discourse is about meditative thinking, not about calculative thinking. The Conversation then goes on to answer the question, What is meditative thinking? and it does so in four steps: (1) Thinking is not willing but waiting, (2) It is letting the realm (*die Gegnet*) be, (3) Letting be is the essence of thinking, and (4) Thinking is thanking. That first point is the key, I believe, that thinking is not willing but waiting. "We are to do nothing but wait,"[9] Heidegger says. I think again of the man who dreamt of two archways, one saying "God with attributes" (Saguna Brahman) and the other "God without attributes" (Nirguna Brahman), and how he interpreted his dream to call, not for choice or will, but for waiting.[10]

What is the realm (*die Gegnet*)? I am reminded of the realm in stories, like Tolkien's Middle Earth or Patricia McKillip's Realm of the High One. Heidegger is using an old word here, *die Gegnet*, used nowadays only in South German dialect, instead of *Gegend*, the current word for region. Translators have used the rather cumbersome phrase "That-which-regions," but I think it is adequately rendered by the word "realm." "An enchanted region," Heidegger calls it, "where everything belonging there returns to that in which it rests."[11] That does indeed sound like the realm of story, the realm of what we can tell. And if thinking is letting the realm be, it means letting everything belonging there return to its rest. I expect it is like thinking you lost someone or something, or even that you lost everyone and everything, and then realizing you never lost what you thought you lost—that is letting it all return to its rest.

If "we can know more than we can tell," it is perhaps in letting all we can tell return to its rest. I think of the Neoplatonic vision of the One, the emanation of all from the One, and the return of all to the One. Thinking as letting be is then letting all come from the One and return to the One and thus letting all return to its rest. I find a peace in the vision itself as if the vision were itself a realization of the return (*epistrophe* in Greek). Thinking as letting be is realization and thus it does make sense to say letting be is the essence of thinking. It is a realization of the One, a realization of the emanation of all from the One, and a realization of the return of all to the One. Talking this way, though, I have left Heidegger behind, and instead of going back to the beginning of Greek thought as he does, I have gone to the end, to what Pierre Hadot calls "the simplicity of vision."[12]

Why go back to the beginning? Why go on to the end? There is a circle here, where beginning and end coincide, and that is "the simplicity of vision" in the end. It is a vision of the Many coming from the One and returning to the One. "Thinking is thanking" then, *Denken ist Danken,* when we realize the circle, that all comes from the One and all returns to the One. Nietzsche's idea of "the eternal return of the same"[13] has the circle without the One, for to him "God is dead." The thanking becomes empty then, becomes "thanking which does not have to thank for something," Heidegger says, "but only thanks for being allowed to thank."[14] Or maybe it is thanking *that* the world is, not for *how* it is, thanking for being, and that in turn can bring us back again to the One, to an eternal return that is *epistrophe,* return to the One.

"Thought does what being does: it lets beings be. Their nature, *Gelassenheit,* is the same,"[15] Reiner Schürmann says, comparing Heidegger and Meister Eckhart. Letting be is the essence of thinking, that is, and also the essence of being. I can see where this is leading with Nietzsche's "God is dead." It leads to Meister Eckhart's *Esse est Deus,* "Being is God."[16] Being that lets beings be is "God without attributes" (Nirguna Brahman), and "God is dead" is "God with attributes" (Saguna Brahman). Yet I can also see the point of not making this choice and instead waiting on God, as thinking is not willing but waiting, and "we are to do nothing but wait." That means entering "the cloud of unknowing in the which a soul is oned with God." It means letting God reveal God to us, and letting God reveal us to us. Here again there is letting be. It is letting be letting be.

One who is detached "experiences such a joy that no one would be able to tear it away from him," Schürmann says, interpreting Meister Eckhart, but such a one "remains unsettled," for one "who has let himself be, and who has let God be, lives in wandering joy, or joy without a cause."[17] Being heart-free then means letting oneself be and letting God be. This way of talking, that being lets beings be, and thinking lets beings be, seems to go with a way of living, letting oneself be and letting God be, that is living in joy, the wandering joy of a journey with God in time. It is the joy of the love of God, joy at the thought of God, as Spinoza says, joy at the thought of being on a journey with God. The way of talking seems for the most part to be a way of turning nouns into verbs, like Hopkins saying "the just man justices."[18]

"Time is what changes and diversifies itself," Meister Eckhart says, "eternity remains simple."[19] Coming from the One is coming into the change and diversification of time, returning to the One is returning to simplicity. Thus letting oneself be and letting God be, becoming heart-free, is returning to simplicity. The joy at the thought of God that is the love of God is the joy of the return, and it participates in eternity, is a taste of eternity. At times when "the mystery of encounter" is at low tide, when friends seem to have forgotten you, the simplicity feels like nothingness, *nada nada nada,* "nothing nothing nothing." The other side of the nothingness, though, is the return, and the vision of the great circle, *mone, proodos, epistrophe,* the One, the emanation, and the return, not the empty "eternal return of the same" but the fullness of return to the One. It is then *todo y nada,* "All and Nothing."

"We seek the unconditioned everywhere," Novalis says, "and only ever find conditioned things."[20] Our seeking, though, is the element of transcendence in us, the restlessness of our heart until it rests in God. Letting be is rest in restlessness, and that is letting ourselves be and letting God be. It is Yes to transcendence and to the transcendence of longing. It is Yes to seeking the unconditioned everywhere and to only ever finding conditioned things, but the peacefulness of that Yes is a finding after all. It is thinking insofar as it is seeking, and it is thanking insofar as it is finding. Thinking is thanking, seeking is finding when it comes to transcendence, and still "we seek the unconditioned everywhere and only ever find conditioned things." Rest in restlessness is like the poise of a gyroscope, and yet it is a peace of mind and heart and soul.

Eternal rest, *Requiem aeternam* as in the Requiem Mass, is it rest in restlessness? "In place of death there was light," Ivan Ilych's experience, may be the key to those sayings in the Gospel of John that if one keeps the words of Christ, "the words of eternal life," one "shall never see death."[21] One shall never see death but in place of death there will be light. I take it this does not mean I will not go through death. It means rather that I *will* go through death, seeing in place of death life and light and love. Eternal rest then means seeing life and light and love. If "we all have within us a center of stillness surrounded by silence," it must mean resting in that center of stillness and being surrounded by the silent presence of God. But that is already possible now in the midst of life before death. If it is like the poise of a gyroscope during life, or like the quiet eye of a storm, it must keep that poise in dying, still be that quiet eye when in place of death there is light.

Requiem aeternam dona eis Domine, "Eternal rest grant unto them O Lord," *et lux perpetua luceat eis,* "and let perpetual light shine upon them." Those are the opening words of the Mass for the Dead. I gather, though, that eternal rest and perpetual light are actual experiences that take place in letting go of everyone and everything in dying. Letting be in dying, it seems, takes the form of letting go and letting God. Eternal rest goes with letting go, perpetual light with letting God. I think of Mozart composing his *Requiem* in his own last days, described in Peter Shaffer's play *Amadeus,* anything but rest and light. Yet in the music there is indeed the rest and the light.

Requiescant in pace, "May they rest in peace," the ending of the Requiem Mass, comes true already in dying in the act of letting go of everyone and everything. There is "the inclination to retirement,"[22] as Festugiere calls it in his *Personal Religion among the Greeks,* and there is also the equal and opposite inclination to hold on. I can see and feel the latter in my own continuing to teach now in my seventies, and I can see and feel the former in my own attraction now to the contemplative life. We have the life of action in our present society but the life of contemplation is largely missing. To let go of everyone and everything can mean to let go of the life of action for the life of contemplation. And what is the life of contemplation? As I understand it, the life of knowing and loving. It is learning to love with all your mind and with all your heart and with all your soul. It is "learning to love" I say with the thought that eternal life begins already on this side of death.

Lux Perpetua, "Perpetual Light," is the title of Franz Cumont's book, originally entitled *After Life in Roman Paganism.*[23] He renamed it *Lux Perpetua* when he came to believe in eternal life. If "faith is seeing light with your heart when all your eyes see is darkness," it is not surprising that he would rename his book for the light you see with your heart. It is true, the experience is more like "catching the light,"[24] seeing things *in* the light rather than seeing the light itself, just as we see things *in* physical light rather than seeing light itself, which can be quite invisible when passing through the darkness of empty space. We see perpetual light when we see things *in* perpetual light, when we see things *sub specie aeterni,* "under the aspect of eternity." So "The contemplation of the world *sub specie aeterni* is its contemplation as a limited whole,"[25] Wittgenstein says. Letting go and letting God lets the world be a limited whole.

All of this comes together in the contemplative life, letting be as essence of thinking, of thanking, even of being, as letting go in dying. And if the letting go of everyone and everything in dying is a passing from active to contemplative life, then clearly dying is a passing into new life. What is more, if philosophy, the pursuit of wisdom, is a "practice of dying,"[26] as Socrates says, according to Plato, then vice versa the practice of letting go of everyone and everything in dying is a pursuit of wisdom, of eternal vision, *eternal visao* as I heard it called at the Church of the Poor Devil on the Amazon.[27] "In place of death there was light," and I want to think of it as "perpetual light" (*lux perpetua*) and as "eternal vision" (*eternal visao*). I think of Goethe's last words "More light!" and what he says in *Elective Affinities,* "It may well be that one day the inner light will come forth out of us, so that we will no longer need any other light."[28]

Light in place of death is enlightenment and guidance and assurance, as the Quakers say of the inner light. There is an enlightenment in life opening up before you all the way to death, there is a guidance there, an assurance, but "In place of death there was light" places death behind you instead of in front, as in the words "One who hears my word and believes on him who sent me has everlasting life and shall not come into condemnation but is passed from death to life."[29] The enlightenment here is in the realization I have everlasting life; the guidance is in hearing the words of eternal life and believing in the God of Jesus; and the assurance is in knowing I shall not come into condemnation but have passed from death to life. This is faith, "seeing light with your heart when all your eyes see is darkness."

When death is in front of you, the enlightenment is that of conscious "being toward death," as Heidegger calls it in *Being and Time,* and the assurance is that of "freedom toward death."[30] I think of a student I had once who came into my office to see me saying "I've found it! I've found it!" and when I asked him what he had found, he said "You accept death, and then you're free!" But where is the moral guidance in this? He was reading and writing about mysticism. I suppose it comes down to Kant's principle, "Act in such a way that you treat humanity, whether in your own person or in the person of another, always at the same time as an end and never simply as a means,"[31] to treat yourself and others as free.

When death is behind you, the enlightenment is the sense of a deeper life that can live on through death, the life of hope and peace and friends and intelligence. The guidance is in the sense of a call to live this deeper life and share this deeper life with others. And the assurance is in overcoming the fear that goes with death in front of you,

I have a sin of fear, that when I have spun
My last thread, I shall perish on the shore;

Swear by thyself, that at my death thy Son
Shall shine as he shines now, and heretofore;
And having done that, thou hast done,
I fear no more.[32]

A New Relation to Everyone and Everything

Letting be and openness to the mystery, according
to Heidegger, puts us into a new relation to everyone and
everything. It is, he says, a new relation to earth ("a new autochthony").[33] I am reminded of the new heaven and new
earth promised in the New Testament. According to this
idea of a new relation to everyone and everything, the new-
ness would be in our relationship to heaven and earth. The
old relationship goes with death in front of us, I suppose,
the new with death behind us and in place of death light in
front of us. And the light, I suppose, is the inner light en-
lightening and guiding and assuring us. If the old relation
is "being toward death," the new is being toward life, toward eternal life, the being described in "the words of eternal life."

This interpretation of the new relation, I realize, is a
Christian interpretation, more like Meister Eckhart's conception of letting be than Heidegger's, though Heidegger
takes the term *Gelassenheit* from Meister Eckhart. As
for Heidegger, his own stance is implicit in his words "We
are too late for the gods and too early for Being." The in-
between place where we are is characterized by "being
toward death" and "freedom toward death," but the new
autochthony he envisions would be like the old relation
with the gods and the new relation to come with Being. If I
am on the right track, taking Being to be equivalent to "the

mystical" (Wittgenstein), then letting be and openness to the mystery is a relationship to the mystical. It is thereby a relationship with God if we say with Meister Eckhart *Esse est Deus,* "Being is God."

If, on the other hand, we say with Saint Thomas Aquinas "God is not the formal being of all" (*Deus non est esse formale omnium*),[34] then letting be is a relationship with God only as doing what God is doing, as in "Let there be light." The basic argument here is that of Plato's dialogue *Parmenides.* Plato is to Parmenides here as Aquinas is to Eckhart as my own view is to that of Heidegger. Plato argues for "participation" (*methexis*) against Parmenides' view that Being is one. The idea of participation is a central one in the thinking of Saint Thomas too, that God is Being by essence and others are Being by participation as well as the contrast of what we can be by nature and what we can be by participation—it was the subject of my doctoral dissertation in theology.[35] And Plato's critique of Parmenides on Being could also be a critique of Eckhart and of Heidegger on Being, and the concept of participation suggests the alternate view I wish to propose here.

Let us consider then first the view in the poem of Parmenides and the dialogue of Plato, then that of Saint Thomas and that of Meister Eckhart, and finally that of Heidegger and my own vision of participation. Let us begin with "the motionless heart of well-rounded Truth," as Parmenides calls it, or as Heidegger translates, "the stable heart of well-enclosing unconcealment."[36]

If I try to *pass over* to Parmenides and "the motionless heart of well-rounded Truth," what comes to mind is the opening sentence of Dag Hammarskjöld on the Meditation Room at the UN, "We all have within us a center of stillness surrounded by silence." Let us assume then that "the motionless heart of well-rounded Truth" is our "center of stillness surrounded by silence." With this assumption the entire poem of Parmenides makes sense. When we are there in our center of stillness, we see things as they truly are. This is what he calls the Way of Truth or the Way of Being. When we are outside our center, things are distorted. This is what he calls the Way of Opinion or the Way of Seeming. Besides these there is no other way but that of Nothing or Non-Being, which he declares inaccessible to us. But when we are in our center of stillness, there is a unity of focus, there is a stillness, there is a surrounding silence.

Does the unity of focus mean a unity of being, the One rather than the Many? Does the stillness mean rest rather than motion? Does the surrounding silence mean a surrounding nothingness? Parmenides does conclude to a unity of being, the One rather than the Many, to rest rather than motion, and I believe to a surrounding nothingness. But let us consider Plato's argument in his dialogue *Parmenides,* on participation and on the One and the Many.

Plato argues that sensible things participate in forms and forms participate in each other.[37] If I try to *pass over* to Plato, I find the notion of passing over requires a notion of participation. It is participation in something common that allows one to pass over to another. We passed over to Parmenides in virtue of a common center of stillness, that "we all have within us a center of stillness surrounded by silence," taking this to be what he calls "the motionless heart of well-rounded Truth." We pass over to Plato then in virtue of the participation that is required by any passing over, taking this to be what he calls "participation" (*methexis*). What then of Plato's thesis, that forms participate in each other and sensible things participate in forms?

Perhaps this could be a way of construing participation and passing over without thereby assuming the separate existence of forms.

At any rate participation (and passing over, I would add) is an answer, an alternative to Parmenides' view on the unity of being, for participation means the Many as well as the One, the Many participating in the One. I think of the Hedgehog and the Fox, the parable Isaiah Berlin draws from Archilochus, who said "The fox knows many things, but the hedgehog knows one big thing."[38] Berlin uses it to discuss Tolstoy's view of history, saying "Tolstoy was by nature a fox, but believed in being a hedgehog."[39] It is true here too, Parmenides is not just a hedgehog with his Way of Being but also a fox with his Way of Seeming, and Plato is not just a fox with his many forms but also a hedgehog with his forms participating in each other, and I too am not just a hedgehog with my heart's desire, the heart being "a center of stillness surrounded by silence," but I am also a fox with my passing over.

"By the mystery of this water and wine may we come to share in the divinity of Christ who humbled himself to share in our humanity."[40] This prayer from the Liturgy of the Eucharist contains the idea of participation that figures in the thinking of Saint Thomas and Meister Eckhart. Here participation has become an interpretation of Christianity. Passing over is twofold here, in virture of sharing in divinity and in virture of sharing in humanity. If I try to *pass over* to Saint Thomas, I find that participation for him takes the form of knowledge and love, and knowledge he sees as taking things in and love as going out to things. Our sharing in the divinity of Christ is a sharing in his knowing and loving, and his sharing in our humanity is a sharing in our knowing and loving. God's presence in us, according to

Saint Thomas, is in being known and loved. Union with God is ultimately through knowledge, the vision of God, because that is taking God into ourselves while love is going out to God. This is the "intellectualism" of Saint Thomas. During life, though, love takes us further than knowledge, and I imagine the climax of life for Saint Thomas as for Dante is in being caught up in "the love that moves the sun and the other stars."

Sharing in the divinity of Christ, as I understand it, is entering into his relationship with God, the unconditional relation he has with his Father, as he says to Mary Magdalene, "my Father and your Father, my God and your God." Here I am differing with Saint Thomas, who has it that the Lord's Prayer is addressed to all three persons of the Trinity and thus our relationship is uniform with all three.[41] Christ's sharing in our humanity, I want to say, is his going through the turning points of a human life, going into solitude, coming back into the human circle, and facing death, and it is possible for us to *pass over* to Christ in these essential moments of life and death.

Making a distinction between essence and existence, as Saint Thomas does, leads to the question whether God is the existence of all things, for God is the One who gives existence to all things, creating them. Saint Thomas says No, affirming the transcendence of God (*Deus non est esse formale omnium*); Meister Eckhart says Yes, affirming the immanence of God (*Esse est Deus*). For me the transcendence comes to light in the transcendence of longing, that our heart is restless until it rests in God, that our heart's longing always goes beyond every finite object, that if we set our heart on someone or something other than God our heart will go beyond and the relationship will fail. Meister Eckhart too seems to realize all this in his teaching on

Gelassenheit, letting be. Openness to the mystery, the attitude that belongs with letting be, according to Heidegger, may be the answer here, openness to the mystery showing and withdrawing, immanent and transcendent.

Near and far, showing and withdrawing, immanent and transcendent, this same duality appears in the relationship of Christ with his Father and in our participation in his relationship. I think again of that dream of two arcades, one saying Saguna Brahman or God with attributes and the other Nirguna Brahman or God without attributes, and the interpretation of the dream that calls for waiting on God. The waiting is like Saint Augustine's prayer "May I know me! May I know thee!"(*noverim me! noverim te!*).

"Like Straw,"[42] the story of the mystical experience at the end of Saint Thomas' life that led him to say all his writings were like straw, may have been the story of a passing over from God with attributes to God without attributes like the God of Meister Eckhart, who tells of the still desert of the Godhead "where never was seen difference, neither Father, Son, nor Holy Ghost, where there is no one at home, yet where the spark of the soul is more at peace than in itself."[43] I find something something similar in Heidegger's saying, "We are too late for the gods and too early for Being," as if to say we are too late for God with attributes and too early for God without attributes. If I try to *pass over* to Heidegger, I am inclined to take his concept of Being to be equivalent to "the mystical," not *how* things are but *that* they are. But here with the still desert of the Godhead we get into the deep places of "the mystical."

"We all have within us a center of stillness surrounded by silence," the principle we used for passing over to Parmenides and "the motionless heart of well-rounded Truth," can also serve for passing over to Meister Eckhart and the

still desert of the Godhead "where never was seen difference, neither Father, Son, nor Holy Ghost, where there is
no one at home, yet where the spark of the soul is more
at peace than in itself." It can also serve for passing over to
Heidegger and his notion of Being. For myself, though, I
want to interpret the surrounding silence as the presence
of God, the presence of "my Father and your Father, my
God and your God."

My own vision of participation and passing over,
in terms of that prayer "By the mystery of this water and
wine may we come to share in the divinity of Christ who
humbled himself to share in our humanity," is one of sharing in his divinity by entering into his relationship with "my
Father and your Father, my God and your God" and passing
over to him in his sharing in our humanity in solitude and
in the human circle and in the facing of death. It is true,
sharing in the divinity of Christ can be seen in Plato's terms
of the forms participating in each other and sensible things
participating in the forms. What comes to light, though, in
sharing in the divinity of Christ is relation and relationship,
I and thou, or more specifically *I in them, and thou in me,*
as is said in the Gospel of John, rather than *I and it.* When
it comes then to passing over to others, passing over to
others than Christ, passing over takes the shape of entering
into relationship.

There is something here like "the road to I and thou,"
Martin Buber's road "from mysticism to dialogue."[44] In his
earlier period of mysticism Buber comes to the ambiguous
conclusion, "We listen to our inmost selves—and do not
know which sea we hear murmuring."[45] We do not know
whether it is the sea of God with attributes or the sea of
God without attributes. But in his later period of dialogue
he comes to an *I and thou* relationship with God, and I

myself come to a Christian vision of the same thing, *I in them, and thou in me.*

So in letting go of everyone and everything in death we come to a new relation with everyone and everything, and the new relation is an *I and thou* relationship. It is a letting be and an openness to the mystery. The letting be (*Gelassenheit*) is a relation to everyone and everything belonging to one's life, a relation of forgiveness (*Prosti*) and farewell (*Propusti*). The openness to the mystery of eternal life is a relation to everyone belonging to one's life on the other side, "the company of immortals,"[46] as Wendell Berry calls them. And the letting be and the openness to mystery is a relation to God where the unknown in death goes from being *it* to being *thou.*

I in them, and thou in me, the Christian vision of eternal life, is a matter of indwelling, Christ dwelling in us and God dwelling in Christ. I think again of Polanyi on "the tacit dimension," and his saying "we can know more than we can tell," and his explanation in terms of indwelling. We can know more than we can tell by dwelling in the particulars of what we know, he says. And so it is here. "We listen to our inmost selves—and do not know which sea we hear murmuring," but by dwelling in the particulars we come to know "I in them, and thou in me." How so? We appropriate the God of Jesus, let his Father be our Father, his God our God, and thus we find him dwelling in us and God dwelling in him. By entering into his relation with God, "the realm of unconditional relation"[47] as Buber calls it, we come to know more than we can tell of the inner sea we hear murmuring.

We know things in terms of our relation to them. So if we have no relation to them, we know nothing of them. To know myself I have to have a relation to myself; to know others I have to have a relation to them; and to know God I have to have a relation to God. "We listen to our inmost selves—and do not know which sea we hear murmuring," Martin Buber's early position, gives way to his later position, *I and thou* over and against *I and it.* My own vision, arising from *I in them, and thou in me,* is of the indwelling of *I in them,* and the indwelling of *thou in me.* The indwelling of *I in them* is that of Christ in us and goes with our passing over to him in solitude and in the human circle and in the facing of death. The indwelling of *thou in me* is that of God in Christ and goes with our making his God our God.

Is this indwelling of Christ in us and of God in Christ a dwelling in the particulars of what we know? "Lord, how is it that you will manifest yourself to us, and not to the world?" a disciple asks in the Gospel of John. "If a man loves me, he will keep my word, and my Father will love him, and we will come to him and make our home with him,"[48] Jesus answers. Loving Christ and keeping his words, "the words of eternal life," I take it, is dwelling in the particulars of what we know of him, and his dwelling in us is the reciprocal of our dwelling in him. We dwell in him, passing over to him and entering into his relationship with God, and so he dwells in us and his God dwells in us.

DEEP RHYTHM

The capacity to speak of God comes only when
the march of time is forgotten, as it is forgotten in
plainsong.

—Paul Griffiths

"It is a truism that Western music since the Renaissance has been about man, about beings whose existence in time is short, directed and hopefully progressive,"
Paul Griffiths says. "The capacity to speak of God comes
only when the march of time is forgotten, as it is forgotten
in plainsong."[1] The timelessness of Messiaen's music, he is
saying there, is like the eternity that can be felt in plainsong. There is no measured rhythm there in plainsong but
only a deep rhythm, a free rhythm.

What can it mean to say "the march of time is forgotten"? There is a "cloud of forgetting" that goes with "the
cloud of unknowing" ("in the which a soul is oned with
God"),[2] and I have come to believe the forgetting is not so
much a literal forgetting as a letting go, a letting go of sadness, a letting go of the sadness that goes with the march of
time. I think again of a moment in my own life when I was

on the Amazon and I asked a sister there if the people I was meeting were really as happy as they seemed. "They can be sad for a day," she replied, "but they can't hold on to sadness." It was then I began to understand the "cloud of forgetting." The sadness, I am seeing now, is linked to the march of time. It is the sadness of mortal existence, like the song of the Riders of Rohan that Tolkien speaks of, "laden with the sadness of mortal men."[3]

What then is this deep rhythm, this free rhythm? There can be joy in the march of time as well as sadness. Both are there in Mozart's music, mostly sunny but melancholy in his G minor compositions. Joy is present in time when time is full of eternity, as in the sense of life as a journey with God in time. In plainsong there is no pulse, no beat, but there is the rhythm of the words. So too in a journey with God in time there is no counting of time but instead a living in the presence in the present. "If we take eternity to mean not infinite temporal duration but timelessness, then eternal life belongs to those who live in the present,"[4] Wittgenstein's saying, I want to modify, as I have been saying, to this, *eternal life belongs to those who live in the presence.*

Living in the presence is what I find in Messiaen's best-known work, composed and performed in a German prison camp in the Second World War, *Quartet for the End of Time.*[5] It is an apocalypse echoing that of Saint John at the end of the New Testament. The score is dedicated in homage to the Angel of the Apocalypse who lifts his hand to heaven saying "There will be no more time." And the music was performed before an audience of five thousand prisoners by a violinist, a clarinetist, a cellist, and Messiaen himself on the piano, in one of the darkest times of the war.

In dark times the message "There will be no more time" is good news. "Never have I been heard with as much attention and understanding," Messiaen said.[6] Living in the presence is the theme of the eight movements with the figures that appear, the sea of crystal, the angel, the birds, the seven trumpets, the rainbows, and Jesus eternal and immortal.

I began in the opening chapter ("A Question of Heart's Desire") with the image of deep rhythm as a pulse like the heartbeat, but now I am using the image of free rhythm in plainsong, where rhythm is not measured out but is that of the words. The change of images goes with a change of focus from the heart's desire to God. When you are thinking of your heart's desire, it is natural to think of the rhythm of life in terms of the heartbeat. When you are thinking of God, "the march of time is forgotten," and time becomes, in Plato's terms, "a changing image of eternity," a changing image of the timeless. The transcendence of longing, "our heart is restless until it rests in thee," is the way from the one to the other, from heart's desire to God.

My own quest of eternal life began when I saw my youth passing, around the age of thirty. I went on a Gilgamesh quest through history, testing all the historic responses to death such as having posterity, doing memorable deeds, running the gamut of experience, and accepting death and becoming free. But the only adequate answer I found was in "the words of eternal life" in the Gospel. The question of heart's desire, as I saw it then, was "If I must die someday, what can I do to satisfy my desire to live?" I tried each of these answers on the question, posterity, memory, experience, simple acceptance, but none of them could stand up to "the words of eternal life." I didn't read Kierkegaard until later, but when I read him I saw I wanted to be a "knight of faith" rather than a "knight of infinite resignation."

There is, nevertheless, "the riddle of eternal life," as I call it here, an expression I am getting from Wittgenstein saying "Is a riddle solved by the fact that I survive forever? Is this eternal life not as enigmatic as our present one? The solution of the riddle of life in space and time lies *outside* space and time."[7] Well, he is saying a riddle is *not* solved by my living forever, and yet he is saying the riddle of life is solved *outside* space and time! I suppose this last is something like saying "The capacity to speak of God comes only when the march of time is forgotten." Eternal life is not endless time, he is saying, but timelessness, and timelessness is living in the present. But again, I would say, it is living in the presence or living in the presence in the present. The presence, as I understand it, is the presence of God as known in knower, loved in lover.

As I understand it then, the riddle of eternal life is this, Is eternal life only symbolic immortality, or is it something more than symbolic? Certainly there is a metaphor here, the three great metaphors of the Gospel of John, life and light and love. I take it, though, that "The love is from God and of God and towards God," as the old man of the desert said to Lawrence, and thus the life too and the light is "from and of and towards." What we have here then is a relationship, a real relationship with God. Thus the saying in the Gospel of John, "And this is eternal life, that they know thee the only true God, and Jesus Christ whom thou hast sent."[8]

If eternal life is timelessness, living in the presence in the present, how is it embodied in time? In the road that goes ever on, I gather, as in Tolkien's song "The Road Goes

Ever On." Deep rhythm here is that of time as "a chang-
ing image of eternity." Tolkien's song and his song cycle,
The Road Goes Ever On, words by Tolkien and music by
Swann, has ordinary measured rhythm except for the song
"Namarie (Farewell)" in the cycle which Tolkien himself
hummed to Swann as a Gregorian chant.[9] The free rhythm
of that song suggests the free rhythm or deep rhythm of actually walking with God in time. I think again of Enoch in
Genesis, "Enoch walked with God, and he was not, for
God took him." And I think of the Buddha's final words to
his disciples, "Walk on."

With the image of walking on and of a road that goes
ever on, however, we have reintroduced the idea of endless
time. We can combine endless time and timelessness by
taking them as two dimensions of life, a horizontal dimension of time and a vertical dimension of timelessness, the
vertical passing through the horizontal in the present
moment. All the same, there is death and dying along the
horizontal line. The road may go ever on, but I cannot go
ever on, and that is what Bilbo sings,

> The Road goes ever on and on
> Out from the door where it began.
> Now far ahead the Road has gone,
> Let others follow it who can!
> Let them a journey new begin,
> But I at last with weary feet
> Will turn towards the lighted inn,
> My evening rest and sleep to meet.[10]

Sailing into the West then is an image of afterlife in this
perspective, a road that goes ever on and yet a person who
is mortal and weary of life. Tolkien has Frodo and Bilbo sail

into the West with the other Ring-bearers at the end of the story. When the Lady Arwen gives Frodo this gift she says "If your hurts grieve you still and the memory of your burden is heavy, then you may pass into the West, until all your wounds and weariness are healed," and she gives him a white gem on a silver chain and says "When the memory of the fear and the darkness troubles you, this will bring you aid."[11] So the afterlife of sailing into the West has the significance not simply of going on but of healing the wounds and weariness of a mortal existence, and there is in this life already a token of it.

Afterlife indeed can be more than a healing of the wounds and weariness of mortal existence. "In sorrow we must go, but not in despair," Aragorn says in farewell to Arwen. "Behold! we are not bound for ever to the circles of the world, and beyond them is more than memory. Farewell!"[12] There is a deeper life, a life of the spirit, a life of hope and peace and friends and intelligence, and I want to say it can continue into life after death. There is a spiritual adventure, I want to say, a deeper life, a going through death to life.

"Even love must pass through loneliness," Wendell Berry begins his poem "Setting Out,"[13] and that is a good description of the spiritual adventure, following the great circle of love "from and of and towards" God, for there is a furthermost point on the circle, furthermost from God, that you have to pass through to return on the great circle to God. I think of the song "Going Home" based on the slow movement of the New World Symphony. To go home to God I have to pass through the loneliness of that furthermost point. "We go to the Father of souls," Saint Cyril of Jerusalem says, "but it is necessary to pass by the dragon."[14] And I suppose passing through loneliness at the furthermost point on the circle means passing by the dragon. When I am lonely, I am vulnerable, my heart is restless. "He can no longer be at home, he cannot return," Berry ends his poem, "unless he begin the circle that first will carry him away."

There is a road taken and a road not taken in life, as Robert Frost has it in his poem "The Road Not Taken." If my road taken is that of the great circle of love from God and of God and towards God, it would seem to encompass any road not taken. When love passes through loneliness, though, a road not taken can emerge and begin to haunt me on my road taken. What then? The answer, it seems, is for the road not taken to rejoin the road taken, as in Isak Dinesen's story "Babette's Feast" where it is said *grace is infinite . . .* See that which we have chosen is given to us, and that which we have refused is also and at the same time granted to us. Ay, that which we have rejected is poured upon us abundantly."[15]

But how does the road not taken in life rejoin the road taken? It rejoins, I believe, if the road taken is that of the great circle of love, for it is there on the great circle that grace is infinite. "He used often to say there was only one Road," Frodo says of Bilbo, "that it was like a great river: its springs were at every doorstep, and every path was its tributary."[16] That one road, if we take it to be the great circle of love, is a road of wholeness, learning to love with all your mind and with all your heart and with all your soul, and even with all your might, like David dancing before the Lord "with all his might." It was for me at first a way of words, and the way of music was left behind as a road not taken, but now it has become a way of words and music, as I learn to love with all my might, and that road not taken has rejoined my road taken along the great circle of love.

Wholeness is not the same as fulfilment, though, and I still have the task of letting be (*Gelassenheit*) and being open to the mystery of loneliness. The letting be and the openness to mystery belong to learning to love with all your soul. I have to let go of my Beatrice, my Laura, the figure in my life who has meant "a new life" to me, as Beatrice did to Dante, as Laura did to Petrarch. Being open to the mystery then is being open to this mysterious life even as I let go of the figure who embodies this life for me. Why? Because of the transcendence of longing, because our heart's longing always goes beyond every finite object, because "our heart is restless until it rest in thee."

This new life, this mysterious life, is a deeper life that can live on through death and after death. If I go with "the thought of the heart,"[17] as Hillman calls it, I start from Saint Augustine's thought, "our heart is restless until it rest in thee," and I am led to an ascent of the mind to God, following the transcendence of longing. I suppose you could say the mind following the transcendence of longing is "the thought of the heart." The first stage in the ascent is the apologia of the person before others, like Newman recounting in his *Apologia* "the history of my religious opinions." The second stage is the meditations of the person before self, like Saint Augustine exclaiming in his *Soliloquies* "May I know me! May I know thee!" And the third stage is the more continuous prayer of the person before God, like Saint Augustine in his *Confessions*, echoing the Psalms.

Deep rhythm is rest in restlessness, and that is what carries you from one stage to another. Rest in restlessness, I have been saying, is like the poise of a gyroscope. The gyroscope is whirling and so it does have a rhythm but its poise is rest in its restless movement. Rest in restlessness is acceptance of the restlessness of the heart. I can simply accept the restlessness of my heart, the restless movement of imagination from one thing to another, or I can accept it "until it rest in thee." If I simply accept my restless heart, I come to something like Leo Bersani and Ulysse Dutoit in *The Forms of Violence*, speaking of "the restlessness of desire"[18] and seeing its unviolent movement from image to image as a remedy for violence. If I accept my restless heart "until it rest in thee," on the other hand, I am led from stage to stage on the ascent of the mind to prayer like Saint Augustine in his *Confessions,* to a circle dance around God.

We speak to God in prayer, but God speaks to us when the heart speaks. I always wondered why Saint Augustine did not continue the style of his *Confessions* in his later works *On the Trinity* and *The City of God,* and I have come to the conclusion here that he is trying to let God speak in these later works. What I have done here is quote the passages in his *Confessions* that anticipate these later works. If we let our own hearts speak, they too may speak of these mysteries. The Trinity comes to light especially when "heart speaks to heart," as in Newman's motto, for the Trinity is essentially relationship. When Christ prays to the Father, when we enter into his relationship with the Father, praying the Lord's Prayer, we seem to be inside the Trinity, as if we were inside a song.

Does the heart speak of the City of God? When we face the decline and fall of the earthly city, as Saint Augustine did, the heart may indeed speak. We could come to that prospect with "infinite resignation," as Kierkegaard calls it, or we can come to it with "faith," a combination of willingness and hope, as Saint Augustine did in *The City of God.* His tale of two cities, like that of Dickens, is then light and shadow, "It was the best of times, it was the worst of times . . ." The light is that of hope, the shadow is that of willingness, where infinite resignation would be willingness without hope, shadow without light. "Unless you hope, you will not find the unhoped-for,"[19] Heraclitus says. Unless you hope in the face of decline and fall, you will not find the unhoped-for city.

"For here we have no continuing city, but we seek one to come," the statement in Hebrews 13:14, suggests that the City of God is part of the mystery of eternal life. Going through death to life means letting be and openness to the mystery of eternal life. The letting be is a letting go of everyone and everything, including the earthly city. Eternal life beginning already in this life, as a deeper life of hope and peace and friends and intelligence, though, suggests that the City of God begins already in this life. And so it is that Saint Augustine tells its story, or reads its story from the Bible. Letting be and openness to the mystery of eternal life seems then to mean letting the things of life be, letting them enter and pass, while staying open to an enduring relationship with God and thus with all else. That enduring relationship would be what Martin Buber calls "unconditional relation."[20]

I think of Pascal's Memorial, all about such a relationship with God. This is how it starts:

FIRE

God of Abraham, God of Isaac, God of Jacob,
not of the philosophers and the savants.
Certitude. Certitude. Feeling. Joy. Peace.
God of Jesus Christ.
"My God and your God."
Your God shall be my God.[21]

I had not realized how close what I have been saying is to what he said there until I looked it up yesterday in order to answer a student's question.

Entering into "unconditional relation" does seem to require letting go of everyone and everything, like going through death to life, and seems to mean entering into a new relation with everyone and everything. FIRE, the word Pascal begins with, FEU in French, suggests the appearance of God to Moses. What is this "unconditional relation"? Speaking of Jesus saying *I,* Buber says "it is the *I* of unconditional relation in which the man calls his *Thou* Father in such a way that he is simply Son, and nothing else but Son."[22] So to enter into that relation I have to let go of everyone and everything else in order to be entirely in that relation. It is then my new relation to everyone and everything. I gather this is the significance of the new name in the New Testament, Simon becomes Peter, Saul becomes Paul. I gather too that entering into this relation means entering into a relation of unconditional love, of loving and being loved.

"God requires the heart,"[23] it is said in the Talmud. There is a letting go and letting God here, letting go of the justification of one's life, as in Tolstoy's story of Ivan Ilych, and letting God's love work in one's life. My own learning to love then comes out of God's loving me. My loving comes of being loved. Thus the primacy here of grace, of God's first loving us. Out of the sense of being loved then I am able to meet the demand of "God requires the heart." So my life becomes a learning to love, with all my heart, with all my soul, with all my might, and as the Gospels add, with all my mind.

If deep rhythm then is rest in restlessness, like the poise of a whirling gyroscope, that rest, that poise enables you to love with all your mind and heart and soul and indeed with all your might, like David dancing before the Lord with all his might. That whirling gyroscope of rest in restlessness is like the circle dance around the One that Plotinus describes, or like the vision of a great circle of life and light and love that is "from God and of God and towards God." Eternal life is the great circle of life and light and love. Deep rhythm is the circular movement of the lifeblood, coming from the heart and returning to the heart, where God is the heart.

"What if the world ends in beauty and golden light?"[24] I asked myself once on walking with a friend in the woods at World's End, a forest reservation near Hingham in Massachusetts. There is an idea of universal reconciliation in the New Testament, a universal reconciliation that is to occur in the end times. The Greek word for it is *apocatastasis,* and the word is actually used in Acts 3:21 ("until the times of reconciliation of all" or "until the times of restoration of all").[25] It is an alternate vision of the end times, alternate to the destructive imagery usually associated with the end. Even the imagery of the Apocalypse of Saint John, usually taken to be an orgy of destruction, can be taken in this way, as Messiaen has done in his *Quartet for the End of Time.* If eternal life is the great circle of life and light and love "from God and of God and towards God," this means an eternal return to God that is a universal reconciliation. And if the deep rhythm of eternal life is a rest in the restlessness of the heart, this means a heart's rest where heart speaks peace unto heart.

A SYMPHONY OF SONGS

I (Songs of the Beginning)

A Dream Dreaming of Us
There is a dream dreaming
    of us,
a larger story we awaken to
upon a mental voyage,
waking us to sleeping
when all things were once at
    one
and we could understand
the language of the sparrows.

The Word in the Beginning
In the beginning was the Word,
and the Word was with God,
and the Word was God.
This was in the beginning with
    God;
all came to be through this,
and without this nothing
    came
that ever came to be.
In this was life,
and the life was the light of
    humankind,
and the light shines in the
    darkness,
and the darkness
has not overshadowed it.

II (Romantic Variations on a Theme of Palestrina)

In the Lost Hills
I met you
dwelling in a human heart;
I found and lost you,
and I lost and found
my soul in the lost hills;
and we shall meet again
as child and child,
and heart shall speak peace
    unto heart.
A human face
and your face in the azure
    light,
a human soul
and your soul of a universe,
and we shall meet again,
face to face,
and heart shall speak peace
    unto heart.
To let friend befriend
and soul besoul,
to let be and be heart-free
and heart-whole,
and we shall meet again,
as friend and friend,
and heart shall speak peace
    unto heart.

Rainbow Dance
I can see
the rainbow in my heart
when all my eyes see
is the dark.

Heart's Desire
An earthly friend I know now
cannot be my Beatrice, my
    Laura,
only Ayasofya can,
for the balance is so delicate
that a butterfly can spread its
    wings
and set off a tornado far away
where there are the balances
    and the periods,
but Wisdom is a strange
    attractor
coming out of chaos where we
    are
and what we hear is mostly
    noise
and we ignore and it disturbs,
but if we listen it is fascinating,
for we are in love with
    Ayasofya,
our changing image of eternity.

III (Songs to Holy Wisdom)

Shadow of God
All hail, wisdom
of silence and the dark,
you are with God
and your bliss is with us
and we are blessed.
All holy wisdom, shadow of
God,
be with me,
always at work in me.

Ayasofya

NOTES

Preface

1. Ludwig Wittgenstein, *Tractatus Logico-Philosophicus*, trans. C. K. Ogden (New York: Dover, 1999), p. 106 (#6.4311). See *Some Folk Say,* an anthology by Jane Hughes Gignoux (New York: Foulketale, 1998) where clearly death *is* an event of life, death *is* lived through.

2. T. E. Lawrence, *Seven Pillars of Wisdom* (Harmondsworth, UK: Penguin and Jonathan Cape, 1971), p. 364. See my discussion in my *Reasons of the Heart* (New York: Macmillan, 1978; Notre Dame, Ind.: University of Notre Dame Press, 1979), p. 1.

3. Wendell Berry, *The Wheel* (San Francisco: North Point, 1982), p. 26 (opening line of "Setting Out").

4. Saint Augustine, *Confessions,* trans. Henry Chadwick (Oxford/New York: Oxford University Press, 1992), p. 3 (bk. 1, chap. 1).

5. *The Notebooks of Joseph Joubert,* ed. and trans. Paul Auster (San Francisco: North Point, 1983), p. 180 (Joubert quoted by Maurice Blanchot).

6. T. S. Eliot, *Four Quartets* (New York: Harcourt Brace Jovanovich, 1971), p. 15 (line 62ff. of "Burnt Norton").

7. Dag Hammarskjöld, "A Room of Quiet: The United Nations Meditation Room" (New York: United Nations, 1971), p. 1.

8. J. R. R. Tolkien, *The Lord of the Rings* (one-volume edition) (London: Allen & Unwin, 1976), p. 87.

A Question of Heart's Desire

1. David Lindsay, *A Voyage to Arcturus* (New York: Ballantine, 1963), p. 36.

2. Ludwig Wittgenstein, *Tractatus Logico-Philosophicus*, trans. D. F. Pears and B. F. McGuinness (London: Routledge & Kegan Paul, 1961), p. 147 (#6.4311).

3. Martin Heidegger, *Being and Time,* trans. John Macquarrie and Edward Robinson (New York: Harper, 1962), p. 311.

4. Ibid., p. 19.

5. Henry Vaughan, "The World" in Robert Penn Warren and Albert Erskine, eds., *Six Centuries of Great Poetry* (New York: Bantam Doubleday Dell, 1955), p. 271.

6. John 6:68 (RSV).

7. Heinrich von Kleist, "On the Marionette Theatre," trans. Idris Parry in *Essays on Dolls* (New York: Syrens/Penguin, 1994), p. 7.

8. T. E. Lawrence, *Seven Pillars of Wisdom*, p. 364. See my discussion in my *Reasons of the Heart*, p. 1.

9. Kleist, "On the Marionette Theatre," p. 3.

10. 2 Samuel 6:14 (RSV).

11. Kleist, "On the Marionette Theatre," p. 12.

12. T. S. Eliot, *Four Quartets* (New York: Harcourt Brace Jovanovich, 1988), p. 28 ("East Coker," line 128).

13. Spinoza, *Ethics,* trans. G. H. R. Parkinson (London: Dent, 1989), p. 209 (bk. 5, prop. 15).

14. Genesis 5:24 (RSV).

15. From George Herbert's poem "The Call," set to music by Ralph Vaughan Williams in his song cycle *Five Mystical Songs* (1911).

16. 1 Peter 3:11 (KJ).

17. Maxim Gorky, *Reminiscences of Tolstoy, Chekhov and Andreev,* trans. Katherine Mansfield, S. S. Koteliansky, and Leonard Woolf (London: Hogarth, 1948), p. 23.

18. Plotinus, *Enneads* 6:9 in A. H. Armstrong, trans., *Plotinus,* vol. 7 (Cambridge, Mass.: Harvard University Press, 1988), pp. 333 and 335.

19. Plotinus, ibid., p. 344 (Armstrong translates "escape in solitude to the solitary" but notes that the usual translation is "flight of the alone to the Alone"). See my discussion in *The Music of Time* (Notre Dame, Ind.: University of Notre Dame Press, 1996), p. 28.

20. Dag Hammarskjöld, "A Room of Quiet."

21. John 16:28–29 (RSV).

22. See the conclusion of the Eucharistic Prayer I–IV in *The New Saint Joseph Sunday Missal* (New York: Catholic Book Publishing Company, 1974), pp. 30, 34, 38, and 43.

23. Master Eckhart, *Parisian Questions and Prologues* (Toronto: Pontifical Institute of Medieval Studies, 1974), p. 85 ("Existence is God") and p. 101 (the one existence of Christ). Wittgenstein, *Tractatus Logico-Philosophicus,* p. 149 (#6.44) (on the mystical). On the *unum esse* of Christ see Saint Thomas Aquinas, *Summa Theologiae* (Rome: Editiones Paulinae, 1962) (one-volume edition), pp. 1959–1961 (part 3, quest. 17).

24. Martin Heidegger, *Poetry, Language, Thought,* trans. Albert Hofstadter (New York: Harper & Row, 1975), p. 4.

25. See Heidegger, *Discourse on Thinking,* trans. John M. Anderson and E. Hans Freund (New York: Harper & Row, 1966), p. 85.

26. Saint Thomas Aquinas, *Summa Contra Gentiles* (Rome: Desclee/Herder, 1934), pp. 27–29 (bk. 1, chap. 26).

27. See my *Peace of the Present* (Notre Dame, Ind.: University of Notre Dame Press, 1991), pp. 93–95.

28. Wittgenstein, *Tractatus Logico-Philosophicus,* p. 149 (#6.4312).

29. Ibid., p. 149 (#6.5).

30. John 4:24 (RSV).

31. Arthur Zajonc, *Catching the Light* (New York/Oxford: Oxford University Press, 1993).

32. Heidegger, *Discourse on Thinking*, p. 55.

33. Henri Nouwen, *The Inner Voice of Love: A Journey through Anguish to Freedom* (New York: Doubleday, 1996).

34. Dante, *Paradiso* 3:85 (my trans.). I am using the edition by E. Moore and Paget Toynbee, *Le Opere di Dante Alighieri* (Oxford: Oxford University Press, 1963), p. 107.

35. Rainer Maria Rilke, *Selected Letters 1902–1926,* trans. R. F. C. Hull (London: Macmillan, 1946), pp. 392–393.

36. See my *Mystic Road of Love* (Notre Dame, Ind.: University of Notre Dame Press, 1999), pp. x–xi, 104–105, music on p. 106.

37. J. R. R. Tolkien, *The Lord of the Rings*, p. 76.

38. Reiner Schürmann, *Wandering Joy* (Great Barrington, Mass.: Lindisfarne, 2001).

39. *The Soliloquies of Saint Augustine* (bilingual edition), Thomas Gilligan, ed. (New York: Cosmopolitan Science & Art Service Co., 1943), p. 70 (my trans.).

40. *The Cloud of Unknowing and Other Works*, Clifton Wolters, ed. and trans. (New York: Penguin, 1978), p. 46 (the original title of the book).

41. John Henry Newman, *Prose and Poetry,* ed. George N. Shuster (New York: Allyn & Bacon, 1925), p. 116.

42. Patricia A. McKillip, *The Moon and the Face* (New York: Berkley Books, 1986), p. 88.

43. Donne, "A Hymn to God the Father" in John Donne, *The Major Works* (Oxford: Oxford University Press, 1990), p. 333.

44. Mark Benecke, *The Dream of Eternal Life,* trans. Rachel Rubenstein (New York: Columbia University Press, 2002), reviewed by F. Gonzales Crussi, M.D., in *Commonweal* (September 27, 2002), pp. 24–25.

45. Dag Hammarskjöld, *Markings,* trans. Leif Sjöberg and W. H. Auden (New York: Knopf, 1964), p. 89.

46. Tolkien, *The Lord of the Rings*, p. 540.

47. Mozart, *Ave Verum* (KV618) (Mainz: B. Schott's Söhne, 1930) (my trans.).

48. John 17:23 (RSV).

49. See my discussion of these concluding words of *Faust* in my *Music of Time,* p. 7.

50. Saint Augustine, *Confessions,* trans. Henry Chadwick (Oxford: Oxford University Press, 1991), p. 3.

51. Diogenes in *Herakleitos and Diogenes,* trans. Guy Davenport (San Francisco: Grey Fox, 1983), p. 47 (#47).

52. Pascal, *Pensees* 91 (206 in ed. Brunschvicg) in *Oeuvres Completes,* ed. Jacques Chevalier (Paris: Gallimard, 1954), p. 1113 (my trans.).

53. Isak Dinesen (=Karen Blixen), *Last Tales* (New York: Random House-Vintage, 1957), p. 100.

54. Michel Serres, *Genesis,* trans. Genevieve James and James Nielson (Ann Arbor: University of Michigan Press, 1995), p. 138.

55. Hermann Broch, *The Death of Virgil,* trans. Jean Starr Untermeyer (San Francisco: North Point, 1945), p. 482.

56. See William J. Richardson, "Like Straw" in P. J. M. von Tangeren et al., eds., *Eros and Eris* (the Netherlands: Kluwer Academic Publishers, 1992), pp. 93–104.

57. 1 John 1:1 (RSV).

An Answer: The Road that Goes On

1. Robert Bolt, *A Man for All Seasons* (New York: Random House/Vintage, 1962), p. 6.

2. Reiner Schürmann, *Wandering Joy,* p. 102.

3. *The Road Goes Ever On,* music by Donald Swann, poems by J. R. R. Tolkien (Boston: Houghton Mifflin, 1967).

4. Tolkien, *The Lord of the Rings,* p. 87.

5. On "the tension of essences" see Albert Bates Lord, *The Singer Resumes the Tale* (Ithaca, N.Y.: Cornell University Press,

1995), pp. 49 and 62 (cf. Ronelle Alexander in the bibliography, p. 239).

6. Tolkien, *The Lord of the Rings*, p. 73.

7. Lord Acton, Letter to Bishop Mandell Creighton, 3 April, 1887.

8. Albert Lord, *The Singer Resumes the Tale*, p. 62.

9. Wittgenstein, *Tractatus* (Pears and McGuinness), p. 147 (#6.4311).

10. Wittgenstein, *Tractatus*, trans. C. K. Ogden (New York: Dover, 1999), p. 106 (#6.4311).

11. Victor Pelevin, *The Yellow Arrow,* trans. Andrew Bromfield (New York: New Directions, 1993), p. 92. See my discussion in *The Mystic Road of Love*, pp. 112–113 and 119–120.

12. Heidegger, *Being and Time*, pp. 19 and 311, cited above in my first chapter, notes 3 and 4.

13. Heidegger, *The Concept of Time* (bilingual edition), trans. William McNeill (Oxford: Blackwell, 1992), pp. 1E–2E.

14. Plato, *Timaeus* 37d (my translation).

15. Alfred Adler quoted in my *Church of the Poor Devil* (New York: Macmillan, 1982; rpt. Notre Dame, Ind.: University of Notre Dame Press, 1983), p. 80, and *Love's Mind* (Notre Dame, Ind., University of Notre Dame Press, 1993), p. 74, but I haven't been able to locate the saying in Adler's own works.

16. Simone Weil, *Waiting for God*, trans. Emma Craufurd (New York: Harper, 1973), p. 135.

17. Dag Hammarskjöld, *Markings*, p. 159 (1957).

18. Saint John of the Cross, *Dark Night of the Soul*, trans. E. Allison Peers (New York: Doubleday/Image, 1990), p. 34.

19. Deuteronomy 6:5, Matthew 22:37, Mark 12:29–30, Luke 10:27 (RSV).

20. Reiner Schürmann, *Wandering Joy*, p. xx.

21. "This union with God's will is the union I have desired all my life: it is the union I ask the Lord for always and the one that is clearest and safest." Saint Teresa, *Interior Castle* 5:3 in *The Collected Works of Saint Teresa of Avila*, trans. Otilio Rodriguez

and Kieran Kavanaugh, vol. 2 (Washington, D.C.: Institute of Carmelite Studies, 1980), p. 350.

22. See my discussion of "rest in restlessness" in my *Time and Myth* (New York: Doubleday, 1973; rpt. Notre Dame, Ind.: University of Notre Dame Press, 1975), p. 79.

23. See my discussion of this saying in *Reading the Gospel* (Notre Dame, Ind. : University of Notre Dame Press, 2000), p. ix.

24. Beethoven, String Quartet in F Major (Opus 135), ed. Wilhelm Altmann (London: Eulenberg, 1911), p. 20. See my discussion in my *Music of Time*, pp. 81–82.

25. Gabriel Marcel, *Being and Having*, trans. Katherine Farrer (New York: Harper & Row, 1965), p. 167.

26. Kierkegaard uses this term "eternal self" throughout *The Sickness unto Death*.

27. Tolkien, *The Lord of the Rings*, p. 747 (see p. 397).

28. Heraclitus (frag. 18) in Kathleen Freeman, *Ancilla to the Pre-Socratic Philosophers* (Cambridge, Mass.: Harvard University Press, 1957), p. 26 (#18).

29. Jean Giono, *The Man Who Planted Trees*, afterword by Norma L. Goodrich (White River Junction, Vt.: Chelsea Green, 1985), p. 50.

30. Tolkien, *The Lord of the Rings*, p. 1066.

31. Ibid., p. 1067.

32. Michel Poizat, *The Angel's Cry: Beyond the Pleasure Principle in Opera*, trans. Arthur Denner (Ithaca: Cornell University Press, 1992).

33. Edward Lorenz, *The Essence of Chaos* (Seattle: University of Washington Press, 1993), p. 181.

34. J. R. R. Tolkien, *The Adventures of Tom Bombadil* (Boston: Houghton Mifflin, 1963), p. 9.

35. Ibid., p. 19.

36. Tolkien, *The Lord of the Rings*, p. 150.

37. Virgil, *Aeneid* VI, ll. 893–901 as translated by Jean Starr Untermeyer in Hermann Broch, *The Death of Virgil*, p. 262.

38.   Barbara Anderson, "Kierkegaard's Despair as a Religious Author" in *International Journal for Philosophy of Religion* (The Hague: Nijhoff, Winter, 1973), p. 243.

39.   Kierkegaard, *Sickness unto Death* (with *Fear and Trembling*), trans. Walter Lowrie (New York: Doubleday/Anchor, 1954), p. 182.

40.   Wittgenstein, *Tractatus* (Ogden), p. 107 (##6.44, 6.45, and 6.522).

41.   Tolkien, *The Lord of the Rings*, p. 74.

42.   Ibid., p. 954.

43.   Wittgenstein, *Tractatus* (Ogden), p. 106 and (Pears and McGuiness), p. 147 (6.4311).

44.   Helen Luke in an unpublished essay on "Choice in the *Lord of the Rings*" (Apple Farm Group Discussions, Three Rivers, Michigan), quoted with her permission.

45.   Patricia McKillip, *Riddle-Master* (New York: Ace, 1999), p. 179.

46.   Tolkien, *The Lord of the Rings*, pp. 1011 and 1015.

47.   Ibid., pp. 1068–1069.

48.   Ibid., p. 1100.

49.   Ibid., p. 210.

50.   Wittgenstein, *Tractatus* (Ogden), p. 107 (#6.45).

51.   Tolkien, *The Lord of the Rings*, p. 58.

52.   Paul Claudel, *Theatre* (Paris: Gallimard, 1965), vol. 2, p. 214. See my discussion of Claudel's words in my *Peace of the Present,* pp. 43–44.

53.   See Rilke cited above in my first chapter, note 35.

54.   See my discussion in my *Mystic Road of Love*, pp. 137–141.

55.   Cf. above, note 4.

56.   Stephen Leacock, *Nonsense Novels* (New York: Dodd, Mead, 1949), p. 60.

57.   My translation of

Haec tua sunt, bona sunt, quia tu bonus ista creasti,
Nil nostrum est in eis nisi quod peccamus amantes,
Ordine neglecto, pro te quod conditur abs te.

in Saint Augustine, *City of God,* bk. 15, chap. 22. I am using the Loeb edition by Philip Levine, vol. 4 (Cambridge, Mass.: Harvard University Press, 1966), p. 544. See my *Love's Mind,* p.112.

A Spiritual Journey

1.   Joanna Field (Marion Milner), *A Life of One's Own* (Los Angeles: J. P. Tarcher/Houghton Mifflin, 1981), p. 89.

2.   Robert Frost, *The Road Not Taken and Other Poems* (New York: Dover, 1993), p. 1.

3.   Isak Dinesen (Karen Blixen), *Anecdotes of Destiny* (New York: Vintage, 1985), p. 60.

4.   Tolkien, *The Lord of the Rings*, p. 76.

5.   Max Gorky, *Reminiscences of Tolstoy, Chekhov, and Andreev,* trans. Katherine Mansfield, S. S. Koteliansky, and Leonard Woolf (London: Hogarth, 1948), p. 23.

6.   Ezra Pound, *Confucius* (New York: New Directions, 1951), p. 198.

7.   1 Peter 3:11 (KJ).

8.   René Girard, *Things Hidden since the Foundation of the World,* trans. Stephan Bann and Michael Matteir (Stanford, Calif.: Stanford University Press, 1987), p. 328.

9.   Genesis 3:5 (KJ).

10.   Tolkien, *The Lord of the Rings,* pp. 84 and 113.

11.   Ibid., p. 288.

12.   Ibid., p. 982.

13.   Ezra Pound, *Confucius,* pp. 27 and 29.

14.   Tolkien, *The Lord of the Rings*, p. 439.

15.   William Nicholson, *Shadowlands* (New York: Penguin, 1991).

16.   John Paul II, *The Theology of the Body* (Boston: Pauline, 1997).

17.   Heinrich von Kleist, "On the Marionette Theatre," p. 3.

18.   See my discussion of these words of Saint Thomas in my *Road of the Heart's Desire* (Notre Dame, Ind.: University of Notre Dame Press, 2002), p. 87.

19. Ibid., p. 19, note 8.

20. Charles O. Hartman, *Jazz Text* (Princeton, N.J.: Princeton University Press, 1991), p. 9.

21. Laurens van der Post, *The Heart of the Hunter* (Harmondsworth, Middlesex, England: Penguin, 1965), p. 139.

22. Ibid., pp. 139–140.

23. See the Mandukya Upanishad in Juan Mascaro, trans., *The Upanishads* (New York: Penguin, 1965), p. 83.

24. David M. Guss, *The Language of the Birds* (San Francisco: North Point, 1985).

25. Ursula LeGuin, *A Wizard of Earthsea* (Berkeley, Calif.: Parnassus, 1968), p. 185.

26. John 6:68 (RSV).

27. See my *Reading the Gospel*, pp. 24–25.

28. Peter Levi, *The Holy Gospel of John* (Wilton, Conn.: Morehouse-Barlow, 1985), p. 7.

29. See my *Reading the Gospel*, p. 25.

30. Palestrina, *Le Opere Complete,* vol. 7 (Rome: Scalera, 1940), pp. 42–46 (the motet) and vol. 29 (Rome: Scalera, 1961), pp. 54–87 (the mass).

31. John 20:17 (RSV).

32. My first song cycle, "Ayasofya," is in my *Love's Mind*, pp. 125–134.

33. Vladimir Solovyov, "Three Meetings," trans. Ralph Koprince in Carl and Ellendea Proffer, eds., *The Silver Age of Russian Literature* (Ann Arbor, Mich.: Ardis, 1975), pp. 127–134. See my discussion in my *House of Wisdom* (San Francisco: Harper and Row, 1985; rpt. Notre Dame, Ind.: University of Notre Dame Press, 1993), pp. 34, 121–123, 125, and 156.

34. My song cycle "The Golden Key" is in my *Music of Time*, pp. 178–183, and "Rainbow Dance" is there twice, on p. 178 and p. 183.

35. I haven't been able to locate the source of this saying but I use it in *The Peace of the Present,* p. 50, and *The Music of Time,* p. 91.

36. My song cycle "The Well at the World's End" is in my *Mystic Road of Love,* pp. 131–136, and the song "Heart's Desire" is on p. 132.

37. The melody is given in *Love's Mind*, p. 48 for the other song "Ayasofya," and the words of the whole song cycle are there on pp. 125–134.

38. See Heinrich Schenker's harmonic analysis of Bach's Prelude in his *Five Graphic Music Analyses* (New York: Dover, 1969), pp. 36–37.

39. The antiphon and canticle are in Morning Prayer of Saturday Week III of the Liturgy of the Hours.

40. Wisdom of Solomon 7:22–23 (RSV).

41. Solovyov, "Three Meetings" in *The Silver Age of Russian Literature,* pp. 128 and 134.

42. Dante, *Paradiso* 31:91–93 in E. Moore and Paget Toynbee, *Le Opere di Dante Alighieri* (Oxford: Oxford University Press, 1963), p. 149.

43. James Hillman, *The Thought of the Heart* (Eranos Lectures) (Dallas: Spring, 1987), p. 24.

44. Ibid., p. 25.

45. Michael Polanyi, *The Tacit Dimension* (Gloucester, Mass.: Peter Smith, 1983), p. 4.

46. Paul Valéry, *Introduction to the Method of Leonardo da Vinci,* trans. Thomas McGreevy (London: John Rodker, 1929), p. 9 and p. 32 (note).

47. Shakespeare, *1 Henry IV,* act 2, scene 4, lines 358–359 in *The Pelican Shakespeare,* ed. Alfred Harbage (Baltimore: Penguin, 1969), p. 685. See my discussion in *Love's Mind,* p. 63.

A Deeper Life

1. Willard Ropes Trask, *The Unwritten Song,* vol. 2 (New York: Macmillan, 1966), p. 80. See my discussion in *The Reasons of the Heart* and *The Music of Time.*

2. William Richardson, *Heidegger: Through Phenomenology to Thought* (The Hague: Martinus Nijhoff, 1963). See Heidegger's preface, ibid., pp. viii–xxiii.

3. See for instance Heidegger, *Discourse on Thinking,* p. 85.

4. *The Soliloquies of Saint Augustine,* p. 70, quoted above in "A Question of Heart's Desire," at note 39.

5. Saint Bonaventure, *The Mind's Journey to God* (*Itinerarium Mentis in Deum*), trans. Lawrence S. Cunningham (Chicago: Franciscan Herald Press, 1979).

6. Saint Robert Bellarmine, *The Ascent of the Mind to God,* trans. T. B. Gent (London: Burns Oates & Washbourne, 1928).

7. Heidegger's preface to Richardson, p. xvi.

8. Master Eckhart, *Parisian Questions and Prologues,* trans. Armand A. Maurer (Toronto: Pontifical Institute of Medieval Studies, 1974), p. 85.

9. Wittgenstein, *Tractatus* (Ogden), p. 107 (#6.44).

10. Saint Thomas Aquinas, *Summa Contra Gentiles* (Rome: Leonine ed., 1934), pp. 27–29 (bk. 1, chap. 26).

11. Wittgenstein, *Tractatus* (Ogden), p. 107 (#6.45).

12. Heidegger, *Parmenides,* trans. Andre Schuwer and Richard Rojcewicz (Bloomington: Indiana University Press, 1992).

13. Wittgenstein, *Tractatus* (Ogden), p. 107 (#6.522).

14. Heidegger, *Discourse on Thinking,* p. 55.

15. John Henry Cardinal Newman, *Apologia pro Vita Sua: Being A History of His Religious Opinions* (London: Oxford University Press, 1964).

16. Ibid., p. iii.

17. Psalm 37:5–6 in *The Psalter* (from the Book of Common Prayer) (New York: Church Hymnal Corporation, 1997), p. 60.

18. Polanyi, *The Tacit Dimension*, p. 4 ("we can know more than we can tell") and pp. 16–19 (indwelling).

19. Søren Kierkegaard, *Fear and Trembling/The Sickness unto Death,* trans. Walter Lowrie (New York: Doubleday, 1954), p. 147.

20. Wordsworth, "Preface to Lyrical Ballads" in *William Wordsworth,* ed. Stephen Gill (Oxford and New York: Oxford University Press, 1990), p. 611.

21. *The Cloud of Unknowing and Other Works,* trans. Wolters, p. 105.

22. *The Upanishads* trans. Juan Mascaro, p. 132 and p. 45. See my discussion in *The Way of All the Earth* (San Francisco: Harper and Row, 1972; rpt. Notre Dame, Ind.: University of Notre Dame Press, 1978), pp. 193–194.

23. Philippians 4:4–7 (KJ).

24. Milton, *Paradise Lost,* ed. John Leonard (New York: Penguin, 2000), p. 3 (bk. 1, l. 25).

25. Saint Augustine, *Confessions,* trans. Henry Chadwick (Oxford: Oxford University Press, 1998), p. xxii (Chadwick's introduction).

26. See above "A Question of Heart's Desire," note 40 (the original title of *The Cloud of Unknowing*).

27. Wittgenstein, *Tractatus* (Ogden), p. 108 (#7).

28. Hans Urs von Balthasar as quoted by Father Dunstan Morrissey in his memoir *To Hear Thoroughly,* ed. Susan Moon (Berkeley, Calif.: Open Books, 1998, 2000), epigraph.

29. I haven't been able to locate the place in Gandhi's writings where I found that saying.

30. Isak Dinesen, *Last Tales,* p. 100. (See above "A Question of Heart's Desire," note 53.)

31. Saint Augustine, *Confessions* (Chadwick), p. 279 (bk. 13, chap. 11).

32. Ibid.

33. Jung, *Psychological Reflections: A Jung Anthology,* ed. Jolande Jacobi (New York: Pantheon, 1953), p. 32.

34. Grimm in a letter to a little girl. See my discussion of Grimm's saying in *The Music of Time,* pp. 63, 82, and 162, of Beethoven's ibid., pp. 20 and 87, and of Newman's in *Love's Mind,* pp. 63–72 (cf. p. 9).

35. Saint John of the Cross, *Ascent of Mount Carmel,* bk. 2, chap. 22 in *Complete Works of Saint John of the Cross,* trans.

E. Allison Peers (Westminster, Md.: Newman, 1953), vol. 1, p. 163.

36. John 3:8 (KJ).

37. Morrissey, *To Hear Thoroughly*, p. 29.

38. Saint Augustine, *Confessions* (Chadwick), p. 222 (bk. 11, chap. 2).

39. George Smoot and Michael Barnett, *The History and Fate of the Universe* (wall chart) (Berkeley, Calif.: Lawrence Berkeley National Laboratory, 2003).

40. Edward Gibbon, *Autobiography* (London: Dent; New York: Dutton, 1939), p. 124.

41. Charles Dickens, *A Tale of Two Cities,* ed. Richard Maxwell (New York: Penguin, 2000), p. 5 (opening sentence).

42. Henry Arthur Jones and Henry Herman, *The Silver King* (1882), act 2, scene 4, in Henry Arthur Jones, *Plays,* ed. Russell Jackson (Cambridge: Cambridge University Press, 1982), p. 61.

43. E. E. Cummings, *Complete Poems* 1904–1962, ed. George J. Firmage (New York: Liveright, 1994), p. 554.

44. Hebrews 11:1, 10, 13, 16, and 13:14 (KJ).

45. Rudolf Otto, *Mysticism East and West,* trans. Bertha L. Bracey and Richenda C. Payne (New York: Macmillan, 1972).

46. "Le silence eternel de ces espaces infinis m'effraie" in Pascal, *Pensées* in *Oeuvres Completes,* ed. Jacques Chevalier (Paris: Gallimard, 1954), p. 1113 (#91 = #206 in ed. Brunschvicg).

47. Mendelssohn, *Song without Words,* ed. Jack Werner (New York: Schirmer, 1951).

48. See my appendix "A Note on the Dante-Riemann Universe" to my book *The Mystic Road of Love,* pp. 137–141.

49. Robert Osserman, *Poetry of the Universe* (New York: Doubleday/Anchor, 1995).

Going through Death to Life

1. Tolstoy, "The Death of Ivan Ilych" in *Tales of Courage and Conflict,* ed. Charles Neider, trans. Nathan Haskell Dole (New York: Carroll and Graf, 1985), p. 410.

2. Wittgenstein, *Tractatus* (Ogden), p. 106 (#6.4311).

3. Ibid. (#6.4312).

4. Tolstoy, "The Death of Ivan Ilych," p. 409.

5. Ibid., p. 410.

6. Heidegger, *Discourse on Thinking,* trans. John M. Anderson and E. Hans Freund (New York: Harper & Row, 1966).

7. Genesis 1:3 (RSV).

8. Peter Shaffer, *Amadeus* (New York: Harper & Row, 1980), p. 29 (act 1, scene 8).

9. Heidegger, *Discourse on Thinking*, p. 62.

10. See above "A Deeper Life," at note 37.

11. Heidegger, *Discourse on Thinking*, p. 65.

12. Pierre Hadot, *Plotinus or the Simplicity of Vision,* trans. Michael Chase (Chicago: University of Chicago Press, 1993).

13. Heidegger, *Off the Beaten Track,* ed. and trans. Julian Young and Kenneth Haynes (Cambridge: Cambridge University Press, 2002), p. 251.

14. Heidegger, *Discourse on Thinking*, p. 85.

15. Reiner Schürmann, *Wandering Joy,* p. 200.

16. Master Eckhart, *Parisian Questions and Prologues*, p. 85.

17. Schürmann, *Wandering Joy,* p. xx.

18. Gerard Manley Hopkins, "As Kingfishers Catch Fire" in *Hopkins: Poems and Prose* (New York: Knopf, 1995), p. 18.

19. Meister Eckhart as quoted by Heidegger, *Supplements,* ed. John van Buren (New York: State University of New York Press, 2002), p. 49.

20. Novalis as quoted by Heidegger, *Supplements,* p. 62.

21. John 8:51 (RSV).

22. A. J. Festugiere, *Personal Religion among the Greeks* (Berkeley: University of California Press, 1954), pp. 53–67.

23. Franz Cumont, *Lux Perpetua* (Paris: P. Geuthner, 1949). Cf. his earlier *After Life in Roman Paganism* (New Haven, Conn.: Yale University Press, 1922).

24. Arthur Zajonc, *Catching the Light* (New York: Bantam, 1993).

25. Wittgenstein, *Tractatus* (Ogden), p. 107 (#6.45).

26. Plato, *Phaedo* 67 in B. Jowett, *The Dialogues of Plato,* vol. 1 (New York: Random House, 1937), p. 451.

27. See my *Church of the Poor Devil*, p. 54.

28. Goethe, *Elective Affinities,* trans. R. J. Hollingdale (New York: Penguin, 1971), p. 171 (part 2, chap. 3).

29. John 5:24 (KJ).

30. Heidegger, *Being and Time,* trans. John Macquarrie and Edward Robinson (New York: Harper, 1962), p. 299 and p. 311.

31. Kant, *Grounding for the Metaphysics of Morals,* trans. James W. Ellington (Indianapolis and Cambridge: Hackett, 1986), p. 36 (second section).

32. Donne, "A Hymn to God the Father" in John Donne, *The Major Works,* ed. John Carey (Oxford: Oxford University Press, 1990), p. 333.

33. Heidegger, *Discourse on Thinking*, p. 55.

34. Saint Thomas, *Summa Contra Gentiles* (Rome: Leonine ed., 1934), pp. 27–29 (bk. 1, chap. 26).

35. Dunne, "Saint Thomas' Theology of Participation," *Theological Studies* (1957), pp. 487–512 (a summary of my dissertation).

36. Parmenides, #1 in Kathleen Freeman, *Ancilla to the Pre-Socratic Philosophers* (Oxford: Blackwell, 1962), p. 42, and Heidegger, *Parmenides,* p. 4.

37. *Plato's Parmenides,* trans. and commentary by Samuel Scolnicov (Berkeley: University of California Press, 2003), p. 48.

38. Isaiah Berlin, *The Hedgehog and the Fox* (New York: Simon & Schuster, 1953), p. 1.

39. Ibid., p. 4.

40. A prayer at the Offertory in the Liturgy of the Eucharist. See *New Saint Joseph Sunday Missal* (New York: Catholic Book Publishing Co., 1974), p. 23.

41. Saint Thomas, *Summa Theologiae* (I am using the one-volume edition, Rome: Editiones Paulinae, 1962), p. 1983 (part 3, quest. 23, art. 2).

42. William J. Richardson, "Like Straw: Religion and Psychoanalysis" in P. J. M. van Tongeren, ed., *Eros and Eris* (the Netherlands: Kluwer Academic Publishers, 1992), p. 93.

43. Meister Eckhart as quoted by William James, *The Varieties of Religious Experience* (New York: Mentor, 1958), p. 320. See my discussion in *The Music of Time,* pp. 25–26, and *The Mystic Road of Love,* pp. 120–121.

44. Paul R. Flohr, "The Road to I and Thou: An Inquiry into Buber's transition from Mysticism to Dialogue" in *Texts and Responses* (in honor of Nahum N. Glatzer), ed. Michael A. Fishbane and Paul R. Flohr (Leiden: E. J. Brill, 1975), pp. 201–225.

45. Martin Buber, *Ecstatic Confessions,* ed. Paul Flohr, trans. Esther Cameron (San Francisco: Harper & Row, 1985), p. 11.

46. Wendell Berry, *A World Lost* (Washington, D.C.: Counterpoint, 1996), pp. 150 and 151.

47. Martin Buber, *I and Thou,* trans. Ronald Gregor Smith (New York: Scribner's, 1958), p. 66.

48. John 14:22–23 (RSV).

Deep Rhythm

1. Paul Griffiths, *Olivier Messiaen and the Music of Time* (Ithaca, NY: Cornell University Press, 1985), p. 17.

2. *The Cloud of Unknowing and Other Works*, pp. 66–67 (chap. 5).

3. Tolkien, *Lord of the Rings*, p. 530.

4. Wittgenstein, *Tractatus* (Pears and McGuinness), p. 147 (#6.4311).

5. Olivier Messiaen, *Quatuor pour la fin du temps* (Paris: Durand, 1942).

6. Griffiths, *Olivier Messiaen,* p. 90.

7. Wittgenstein, *Tractatus* (Ogden), p. 106 (#6.4312).

8. John 17:3 (RSV).

9. Tolkien and Swann, *The Road Goes Ever On* (Boston: Houghton Mifflin, 1967), p. vi (from the foreword by Donald Swann).

10. Tolkien, *Lord of the Rings,* p. 1024.

11. Ibid., pp. 1010–1011.

12. Ibid., p. 1100.

13. Wendell Berry, *The Wheel* (San Francisco: North Point Press, 1982), p. 26.

14. Saint Cyril of Jerusalem quoted by Flannery O'Connor, *Mystery and Manners* (New York: Farrar, Straus & Giroux, 1969), p. 35.

15. Isak Dinesen (Karen Blixen), *Anecdotes of Destiny*, p. 60, cited above in "A Spiritual Journey," at note 3.

16. Tolkien, *Lord of the Rings,* p. 87, quoted above as epigraph to "A Spiritual Journey."

17. James Hillman, *The Thought of the Heart*, quoted above in "A Spiritual Journey," at notes 43 and 44.

18. Leo Bersani and Ulysse Dutoit, *The Forms of Violence* (New York: Schocken, 1985), pp. 110–125.

19. Heraclitus (fragment #18) quoted above in "An Answer: the Road that Goes On," at note 28.

20. Buber, *I and Thou,* pp. 66–67, quoted above in "Going through Death to Life," at note 47.

21. Pascal, Memorial in Pascal, *Oeuvres Completes,* ed. Jacques Chevalier (Paris: Gallimard, 1954), p. 554 (my translation).

22. Buber, *I and Thou,* pp. 66–67.

23. See my discussion of this saying from the Talmud (Sanhedrin 106b) in *The Peace of the Present,* pp. 18–19.

24. I ask this question in *The House of Wisdom,* p. 152.

25. See Hans Urs von Balthasar in his preface to *Origen,* trans. and intro. by Rowan L. Greer (New York: Paulist, 1979), pp. xii and xiv, and Karl Rahner, *Karl Rahner in Dialogue,* ed. Paul Imhof and Hubert Biallowons, trans. edited by Harvey D. Egan (New York: Crossroad, 1986), pp. 194–195 on *apocatastasis.*

INDEX

JOHN S. DUNNE

is the John A. O'Brien Professor of Theology at the University
of Notre Dame and the author of nineteen books, including
*The Road of the Heart's Desire: An Essay on the Cycles of Story
and Song* (2002) and *A Vision Quest* (2006), both published
by the University of Notre Dame Press.